An Angel saved my life

An Angel saved my life

And other true stories of the Afterlife

Jacky Newcomb

'THE ANGEL LADY'

HarperElement
An Imprint of HarperCollins*Publishers*
77–85 Fulham Palace Road,
Hammersmith, London W6 8JB

The website address is: www.thorsonselement.com

and *HarperElement* are trademarks of
HarperCollins*Publishers* Ltd

First published by HarperElement 2006

1

A catalogue record of this book is
available from the British Library

ISBN-13 978-0-00-720569-1
ISBN-10 0-00-720569-4

Printed and bound in Great Britain by
Clays Ltd, St Ives plc

Contents

To Anthony … safe in the arms of the angels.

Acknowledgements

So many people helped me with the stories for this book and I want to especially thank Jill Wellington who did so much … again!

I also want to thank everyone who was kind enough to share their amazing stories with me. Without your willingness to share and open your soul there would be no book. Your stories bring joy and hope to many.

Introduction

We now live in a time when it's totally acceptable be a 'BELIEVER' in Spirits and Angels. Be proud to be a member of this ever growing club and go forward with a twinkle in your eye knowing that you are always watched over and guided.

Tony Stockwell

When I first started investigating the angel phenomenon I was bowled over by the incredible stories I'd heard of angel intervention and life-saving experiences. For many people, an 'angel experience' begins a life-long interest in these beings of light. If you believe in angels then angel experiences are 'proof' of their existence. If you don't believe in angels then it's hard to ignore and write off these stories completely. They can't all be coincidences, surely?

Angel experiences have a certain something about them. People say, 'I just knew it was an angel.' There's a feeling or a sense about it which is difficult to explain to anyone else. Usually there is no 'proof' and often the experiences happen when one is alone – perhaps that's part of the magic!

If you are interested in the spiritual side of life then you might not need 'proof' that angels exist at all; I know that I don't. Science after all is limited. Parapsychologists who try to prove that some paranormal events or beings can be measured come up against several difficulties. First of all, we don't really know where to look for angels and secondly, we don't know how to look … even if we did, we don't yet have equipment which could measure their existence. How could we provide such evidence of these celestial beings? Would we even know if we'd actually gathered the proof we were seeking? Science at least is at the point where scientists are saying that, in theory at least, it is possible that these other dimensions and our ability to perceive them are possible, so watch this space!

When I was a young girl I used to wake up night after night and 'see' someone in my room, and I couldn't understand why. My Dad would do the fatherly check and open the curtains, look under the bed and open the wardrobe door. Of course, he never did find anyone but I knew that someone was with me – always. The problem was that no one else could see my guardian and so, for everyone else, he did not exist. But for me he was there.

As I got older I read more about the existence of angels and the afterlife and I realized that my own guardian had been communicating with me the whole time. Many other experiences over the years suddenly seemed to make sense. The warning voices in times of trouble, and the 'gut instinct' which got me out of difficulties and probably saved my life. This was my angel at work.

Encountering an angel in your life is a fairly rare thing for most people. If you are lucky enough to experience an angel it is more likely to occur when you are in a life or death situation or at a time when there seems nowhere else to turn. Angels appear when we call out for them in extreme stress or grief – although this is not always the case. I do believe that we need to give angels permission to help us – at least on some conscious level. We feel them at a deep soul level and we let them know that we want them in our lives.

I would like to share with you some of the hundreds of stories I have received from around the world. Some are bizarre, others are totally unexplainable. Some are comforting and some are … well, I'll let you decide! No scientific experiments have been done here. I believe in the integrity of each and every person who has been kind enough to honour me with the permission to share their very personal and intimate stories here with you. Are these stories real? Absolutely!

But first I must begin with my own psychic experiences. I shared some of these in my book *An Angel Treasury* and so here I continue the tale. Knowing about some of the experiences I have been through myself will give you a little understanding of what I see, and why I see it; and certainly why I think the way that I do.

I am a normal mum of two teenage daughters and certainly not a spiritual guru of any kind, and yet I have experienced the most bizarre paranormal things in my life. Some of these things have just 'happened' to me and others I have sought out along the way to explore my own spirituality and boundaries. These things have been for my own research. You in turn must find your own way along the spiritual path. When I look at the things I have documented in Part 1 about my own path (and I have only written here the mere beginnings of my spiritual travels), I myself find it hard to believe, and yet everything I have shared here is true.

The second part of this book deals with amazing 'angel experiences' I have come across in my research. Angels come in all sorts of disguise. Angel stories fill my books *An Angel Treasury* and *A Little Angel Love* but in *An Angel Saved My Life* I have documented some of the more dramatic experiences I have encountered. Experiences which happened to different people in different parts of the world, and often many years apart, seem to have a similar theme. I am left in no doubt as to the existence of angels. But as always, I'll let you choose for yourself.

The third part of the book looks at the mysteries of the afterlife and at contact through the veils of heaven. Sometimes these experiences blend with the angel stories I have received. At times the stories will blur across the divide and merge between the chapters which I have created, but ultimately that does not matter. I have tried to create some order and 'sort' the stories for you. The natural world does not usually fall into such easy sections! Often when people send their afterlife communication stories to me they called them 'angel stories'. These are, after all, 'angel stories' by another name ...

Be ready to be astounded, as I was and am.

Angels transcend every religion, every philosophy, every creed. In fact Angels have no religion as we know it ... Their existence precedes every religious system that has ever existed on Earth.

Saint Thomas Aquinas

Part 1

CHAPTER 1

My Own Psychic Story

The power of Thought, the magic of the Mind!
Lord Byron

'Mummy, Mummy, there's a man in my room!'

Usually Dad would come in and search under the bed, open the wardrobe and pull back the curtains, as dads do when they are searching for 'monsters in the bedroom' – although of course he never found anyone or anything! Many years later I realized that I was seeing a spirit guardian or angel, and that I have always had this spirit with me, and still do.

Kabam is my own guardian angel or spiritual guide and when I looked back I realized how, like most people, I had experienced psychic and paranormal activity in my 'normal' life. Like most people, this phenomenon was filed away in my mind under the '... that was weird wasn't it ...' moment and I had completely forgotten about it. I truly feel that we are all psychic in one way or another and from time to time we tap into these other realms and alternative states.

When our minds fall into a daydream, when we drop off to sleep, and when we meditate, our minds are in an altered state; a state different to our normal waking consciousness. It is during these times that we are most likely to have supernatural experiences of our own.

I remember having several 'paranormal' experiences as a child. On a family holiday on the Isle of Wight I got into difficulties in the sea (I wrote about this in full in *An Angel Treasury*). A calm presence aided me back to shore; a presence unseen but heard and felt. Had an angel saved my life?

Another day my family and I walked along the windy seaside pier and struggled to stand upright. The wind was so strong and pushed us along and it was enormous fun. My sister and I fantasized about being lifted up by the breeze and floating in the air. Later that night I had a dream so real that I thought I had really spent the evening flying down the pier. Years later I realized that this was called an 'out-of-body experience' (OBE) and after reminiscing with my sister over the holiday we had as children, I realized that the two of us had the same 'dream' memory! We actually had flown down the pier but we did so in our spiritual or astral bodies rather than physically. For me it was the first of many such experiences.

I always read a lot as a child, and as a teenager I had piles of paperbacks stacked up by my bed. One of those books was the groundbreaking work by Dr Raymond

Moody, *Life After Life*. It was piled up amongst the other books which my mum had recently bought from the local jumble sale. Those works included typical teenage reads of the time … things like *Confessions of a Window Cleaner* and pretty well anything by the English romance writer Barbara Cartland! My friends and I shared similar tastes.

Dr Moody's book was very different of course and was not a work of fiction. It had quite obviously been picked up 'by mistake' by my mother, and yet his work, about near death experiences (and the now well-known 'white light and tunnel' experiences that people have at the point of psychical death), was to change the course of my life.

The near death experience is now part of our popular culture. Who hasn't seen *Ghost* with Demi Moore and Patrick Swayze? Patrick of course plays Sam who is murdered in the film, but when he is finally ready to pass over he is taken into the familiar 'white light and tunnel' to heaven.

Millions have had this experience all over the world. With the advancement of medical techniques, many are now literally brought back from the very brink of death. Many have found themselves floating above their body and seeing the white light ahead of them – they know that this light is waiting to take them to the heavenly realms. Of course, not every out-of-body experience is related to near death. Many people have out-of-body experiences where, like me, they had a need to go somewhere or do something which physically they were unable to do at the time. This can cause the spiritual body to leave the physical. A severe shock or trauma can also do the same thing.

But back to the real world ... I remember as a teenager, waking up in the early hours of the morning as an ambulance arrived to take my dad to hospital. When my dad collapsed behind the bathroom door with a stomach ulcer he later swore that he had tried to help my mother open the door from his side, even though he was unconscious at the time. I remember my mum's frustration when she tried to explain to my dad that he had passed out behind the door which basically trapped him inside. Later I understood that the experience he'd had was as an NDE or near death experience as explained by Dr Moody in his book. He too had left his body for just a few moments, and even though he was unconscious, he was still mentally aware.

Oh how I wish that the internet had been around then. My local library didn't really hold the information that I was seeking as a teenager, and I didn't have the money to buy esoteric books, even if I had been able to locate them. It was a frustrating time.

Later when my sister bought the books written by the medium Doris Stokes I devoured them all. There was a distinct lack of material to read on anything remotely 'paranormal', and her work found me very excited indeed.

When my husband and I moved into our second house I often used to wake up at night worried that the next-door neighbour of our semi-detached house would be burgled. Night after night I woke up and would hang my head out of the bedroom window. I became paranoid about it happening. In my mind I could see that it would happen. Then one night my neighbour actually was burgled, and strangely I slept through the whole thing! I often wondered if this had been a premonition of some sort.

When my husband John and I were first married I often used to see spirit people in my room at night, in the way that I had as a child. Sometimes it was one person and on other occasions there were whole crowds of people. My bedroom was fast becoming the local waiting room for spirits. The whole thing frightened me until I shared my experience with a more knowledgeable friend. 'Ask them to go away,' she suggested and I tried it. I was amazed that it worked and I began to get some sleep at last.

All the time I was growing up, I longed to be psychic but of course I already was – we all are, in our own individual way. When my girls were small I used to work in a local pub on a Sunday. Much of the work was boring and as I cleaned tables my mind would wander and I would often pick up very unimportant premonitions of things that might happen later in the day or sometimes in just a few minutes' time.

One day I distinctly heard a question in my head. 'What's in those spray bottles you use to clean the tables with?' In my mind I answered the question but then a few minutes later, a gentleman walked up to the bar and, passing me on the way, stopped to ask me the very same question, which I believe he'd been thinking about just a few minutes earlier, and I, in my daydreaming state, had somehow picked up his thoughts. It was just washing up liquid and water and I'd already rehearsed the answer in my head. This 'day-dreaming' state is the perfect opportunity for us to pick up information psychically or hear messages from our guardian angels.

One of the waitress's jobs in this pub was to make up the complicated ice-cream desserts which we layered with fruit, sauces and cream into tall glasses. I remember one day looking longingly at a particularly delicious chocolate concoction and I clearly heard a voice in my head say, 'There will be a spare one later today and you will be offered it.' Right at the end of the afternoon, one of the waitresses made a mistake and created too many of the chocolate ice-creams and the manager suggested that she offer it to one of the staff. She picked me. No one knew of my thoughts and even I remember mulling over this experience and wondering what the purpose was of such a seemingly useless premonition. I enjoyed the ice-cream just the same …

The thought of the 'useless premonitions' came back to haunt me when some weeks later my sister-in-law telephoned us at home. She had some horrific news for us. Her husband Anthony had died at work. He'd been found dead at the bottom of the hold of the ship where he had been working for Customs and Excise, and it blew the bottom out of our world.

The world literally stood still for several moments as I digested what she had said, and passed the phone over to my stunned husband. Anthony was dead. How could this be? He was a young dad with four children. I immediately went into shock.

I had no idea what to say as denial flooded my brain. My husband immediately packed a bag and drove the two hours to Cardiff so that he could be with his sister. I remember how awful it was to stay home at the time but the girls were small and it was just impractical to travel with them. Strange memories of the year before came flooding back over the next few days ...

Twelve months before I'd had some outlandish psychic predictions which came to me like pieces of a puzzle ... had I had some idea that this terrible thing was going to happen? I remember feeling really shocked one day when I had a vision of jumping out of a plane with a parachute. My mind's eye was focussed on the ground and as it got closer and closer my palms began to sweat. I felt like someone we knew was going to fall and I said so to my husband. It seemed a strange thing to say but it seemed to unlock a psychic doorway and this was just the beginning.

As the weeks went by I became more and more obsessed with the idea that someone was going to fall and die, and when one of my sisters and I spent the day together I talked to her about it too. We stood looking out of my children's bedroom window one day and I actually said to her, 'It's a bigger fall than this,' as if I were searching desperately for what I had been given. I couldn't make any sense of what I was experiencing and of course I didn't want to hear what I was hearing. Then when we took the children to the local swimming pool I looked over the restaurant balcony to the swimming pool below and my palms began to sweat again. 'It's not as high a fall as this,' I said crazily.

I remember another day when we had recently finished decorating our smallest bedroom, and how proud I was. I commented on how my sister-in-law would love to stay in the room. But then I reasoned out loud that this was a ridiculous idea. Why would my sister-in-law come and stay without her husband ... unless he died? I was totally shocked at what I had said. These were just random thoughts mulling through my head, or were they? Why would I say such an awful thing or even think it? I couldn't even fathom such a thing and immediately wiped it from my mind.

Of course, you don't ring someone up and tell them that you have just had the most awful thought about them, and so I pushed the idea to the back of my mind. Later, when I heard the details of the accident over the phone, all the other pieces of the puzzle came together, and I realized that I'd had what amounted to a premonition but without enough information to do anything about it.

We used to visit the family every few months or so but for some reason we had become enthralled with the idea of moving to the Cardiff area where they lived in the three weeks before Anthony died. My husband John was working in Birmingham at the time so it actually didn't make any sense to move out of the area. Nevertheless, we visited and stayed with my sister-in-law and her husband for three weeks in a row whilst we 'house hunted'. I remember on the third weekend, having a conversation with Anthony about the afterlife and I shared with him my knowledge of what happens when you die and go to the 'light'. It was probably the most intimate conversation we had ever had and the last proper conversation we had together. The following week he died.

The whole crazy 'let's move' idea had given us the opportunity to spend some time together before he passed and for that I will always be grateful.

I was at home alone, a few days after he passed. John of course was still in Cardiff. I was in the kitchen when I suddenly felt I was not alone. For just a few moments the energy of the room changed. I momentary saw a streak of light pass my vision. It was nothing definite but I still knew what it was.

'Is that you?' I asked into the air. I called his name. In an instant the energy changed back to normal and I knew I had been visited by Anthony's spirit one last time.

I travelled down for the funeral. Another relative looked after the children and my parents drove me there. Everyone was amazingly 'together and calm' as they celebrated his life with joy. The house was full of people as it had been over the whole week apparently. Later, as John, my sister-in-law and I drove to the church for the funeral, the streets were lined with hundreds of Customs officers. Police were directing the traffic and had to stop cars to let us through. It was a bizarre sight. So many people had lined the streets to show their respects for this well-loved man. We knew that he would be watching down and laughing at the commotion he had caused. We laughed too. It's amazing how human beings have the ability to laugh along with their tears.

After the Mass, we walked to the graveside. My sister-in-law stepped forward. It occurred to me that another adult should be supporting her in her grief, but as my husband was helping to carry the coffin, I understood with disbelief that this role was mine. I was the chief mourner's first support. I became a real adult that day.

We visited most weekends for nearly a year after that. We all wanted to be together as one large family. John attended to many maintenance jobs in my sister-in-law's house, putting up shelves and so on. We cleaned and cleared, almost as if moving the sadness out of the home. One afternoon, after a busy day of maintenance, we sat down for a coffee in the small family room at the front of the house. John had isolated the electrics only moments after the kettle had boiled but as we all sat in the room, the lights flickered on and then off again.

'I thought you switched those off?' I asked, surprised.

'I did! But I'll go and check again,' said John, rushing off to the fuse box. 'Yes, it was switched off but I have pulled out all of the electricity fuses just to be on the safe side.'

But the lights were still on and now began to flicker on and off teasingly! We all laughed that the lights were a message from Anthony, but we still decided to get an electrician in to check before John did any more work with the electricity. By the time the electrician arrived an hour later the lights had switched off. He spent an hour checking wires and cables and then came back to ask us again about the lights.

'Are you sure the lights were on when all the fuses were pulled out?' he queried.

'Yes,' we assured him, several times!

We sent the electrician on his way but were not concerned. We knew who had been messing with the electrics! We'd had a clear signal from the other side. All of these things were creating a drive in me – a need to find out what is going on in these other realms.

All through the next year I remained mad with frustration at my own poor 'psychic skills'. What was the point of picking up premonitions if there was never enough proof or facts to do anything to stop it? I suffered from depression for quite a long time after Anthony died. It was a combination of different things which I felt had triggered this.

My husband worked away from home a lot and later I lost my grandmother, which hit me hard. On the day of the funeral my youngest daughter, who was just two at the time, looked up at the ceiling and said in an excited voice, 'Look Mummy, a fairy man!' I couldn't decide if her vision was an angel or perhaps my grandmother coming to say goodbye. Children do seem to see things that adults cannot.

In less than six months' time it happened again. I received another unwanted forewarning and this time it was much clearer. We had been invited down to the south coast to the fiftieth birthday party of a family friend. We decided to stay overnight as it was a good five hours' drive, and piled our luggage and two small daughters into the car. I closed the front door and walked towards the car. As John began to pull off the drive I had a blinding premonition.

'Stop!' I yelled.

Confusion passed over his face as he asked me what the matter was.

'I think we're going to be burgled,' I yelled.

It was an extreme thing to say but he calmly asked me what I wanted to do. I decided to go back into the house. I checked that all of the windows were locked downstairs and then I rushed up to my bedroom where I had stored a considerable amount of gold and silver jewellery, much of which had been inherited. I often hid it out of sight if we went away, but today I hadn't.

I searched through several jewellery boxes and picked out my favourite pair of earrings and put them on. Then I placed the gold sovereign necklace that my parents had given me for my eighteenth birthday around my neck. I poked through and found the ring which my husband had given me on our engagement and a couple of other rings, followed by three gold bracelets. It was all I could wear in one go and when I had finished I closed the lid and replaced the box on my dressing table. Why did I do this?

My husband was amazed that I hadn't hidden all the jewellery away as I had on previous occasions, but today this felt the right thing to do. We talked in the car about what I had felt and why I had chosen to pick out certain pieces of jewellery. I felt sure that we were going to be broken into when we were away and nothing could convince me otherwise. The conversation continued once we arrived at our friends' home and I told every-one how being burgled would probably leave me feeling unsafe and I would probably go out and buy a dog, and that it was a bad thing for us to do! It was almost as if I had some memory from a moment which had been pre-planned as a lesson in my life. Had I 'seen' this happening as a life choice before I had been born? How did this work?

The next day we began the long drive home and as we pulled onto the front drive our neighbour rushed out to meet us.

'I'm so sorry, you've been burgled,' she said.

We sat in shock for just a moment. I initially stayed in the car with the girls so that John could quickly check the house was safe for the girls to enter. We had no idea what we might find. As soon as he nodded that the coast was clear I came in with the girls and put them to bed. They were too young to really understand but we just mentioned that it was okay as none of their toys had been taken. Then we began to look around at what had happened.

The burglars had climbed in through the kitchen window. Our home looked out onto open fields, and what had once attracted me to the house now became my biggest fear. We were open and exposed. The window catch had been broken and the glass had been smashed.

John boarded up the window and replaced the glass immediately the next day. I insisted he nail it shut, and we never opened that window again. The remaining glass had been dusted for finger prints by the police and the shiny dust was still on the window. I shuddered at the thought of what they might have found. Real people had entered our home. I remember feeling cross that no one had thought to secure the building before our return. It would have been easy for the burglars to have returned for more of our things.

The burglars had walked right to the master bedroom, stopping only to break the lock on a briefcase where they had taken the expensive gold pens John had received as gifts for his twenty-first birthday. In the bedroom they had opened every drawer and every jewellery box and tipped everything onto the bed. These burglars were only looking for specific things and they had picked out every single piece of gold jewellery, and left every single item of silver. I glanced down at my wrist and noticed the bracelets still on my arm. I still had 'one body's worth of jewellery' left.

When the insurance company came to assess the burglary, I had already listed every item that was missing and found out the price of replacing each piece. Seeing the piles of empty jewellery boxes they didn't query the claim and the cheque came a few weeks later. I had already decided that I wouldn't replace any of the pieces but use the money to buy a car and learn to drive. I was determined that this negative experience would have a positive affect on my life. So passing my driving test later was a big healing experience for me. I was able to silently say, 'Thanks for the car.' I never did replace that gold jewellery.

The day after we arrived home, the police came to visit, and one of the things they suggested was that we buy a dog for security. With John's working schedule I was often alone with the girls and it seemed the natural thing to do. I could still hear my words of the previous day: 'We'll probably buy a dog but we shouldn't.' The words echoed in my ear before disappearing into the distance. I'd heard and promptly ignored the warning from my inner guidance.

A couple of days later I bought a dog bowl and a packet of dog food and we made the trip to the local RSPCA dog home to purchase and 'rescue' a dog. With no planning at all we chose a beautiful Collie-cross puppy and after our home inspection from the charity we brought our puppy, 'Shandy', home.

I have never seen such an intelligent dog and he was a fast learner and picked up many tricks, but he was harder work than the children. He couldn't be left for a minute and totally destroyed the kitchen and large parts of the house, as puppies do. He ate his way through the kitchen cupboards and the kitchen chairs. We decided to make him a kennel outside but he ate that too, and then he ate his way through the garden fence and later dug his way under. When he was a little bigger he jumped over the fence and escaped.

Why had I not listened to my own premonition about the dog? The guidance I had heard was clear enough but we'd bought the dog just the same. I was no longer able to cope and John began walking the dog on his own. Shandy regularly slipped his lead and would disappear for two hours or more with John walking for miles calling his name. One day he ate another large hole in the garden fence and followed a woman home on her bicycle, all the way to the next village. He escaped three times that week and twice we phoned the police to see if anyone had handed him in because we just did not know what else to do.

When John was working away the following week I remember trying to take Shandy for a walk in the pouring rain. I had to push the girls in a double buggy, and Shandy almost pulled us all into the road. I came home wet and tired and cried all the way home. Later when I fed Shandy, my eldest daughter Charlotte walked past him and he snapped at her. I just screamed hysterically and shut him in the kitchen.

He was a beautiful dog but the mistake in taking him on was ours. When you purchase a dog from the RSPCA, you agree to return it if there is a problem, so we took him back. On the day we handed him over I cried for several hours. I felt such a failure and I felt so ashamed. When they rang us a few days later to say that he had been taken home by a family who lived on a farm and wanted him as a working dog I cried some more. He was so intelligent he would love it. It was a difficult time and the guilt I felt was unbelievable.

Anthony had died, and so had my grandmother. We had been burgled and I had given up my dog and all this happened in a very short time. It was no wonder that I slipped into a deep depression but had no idea what was happening to me. I didn't know anyone who'd suffered from depression and so I had no one to discuss it with. I was good at keeping up appearances and although the house was in a serious mess, inside and out I was good at hiding the worst of it when people came around.

I used to have an ironing cupboard and all the clean washing would get thrown in there. I was too ill to do more than look after the children each day and breathed a sigh of relief as I dropped the eldest off at playgroup twice a week. I usually managed to hide my tears. One day I remember one of the mothers walking up to me outside the playgroup to see if I was okay. I'd been crying for several hours and my make up couldn't hide it any longer. She walked back home with me for coffee and it was the first time I was able to talk about how I was feeling.

I realized that something serious was wrong and finally made a trip to the doctor. The doctor placed me on antidepressant tablets. The tablets made me feel like I was living in a fog, but they did help a little. The psychic experiences had gone (probably as a result of the antidepressants) but I still felt unable to do anything other than the bare minimum of work in the home. Everything we ate came straight out of the freezer. I didn't cook – I just warmed things up. I felt numb and only half on the planet.

I remember feeling as if I had a ball and chain around my ankle. I couldn't manage even the simplest of tasks. I spent hours sitting on the sofa watching television and when John came home at night he would often enquire politely about my day. I would make something up because I couldn't remember doing anything at all. What did I do? I day-dreamed my life away ...

Later, I began working as a temp and did occasional work as a personal assistant or receptionist in many of the large companies in our local brewing town. I was able to cope with the short-term jobs and it was great to get out of the house again. As soon as a job became a little longer, though, I started to get into difficulties. I just couldn't manage, even though I was offered permanent positions constantly. I knew that I would not be able to keep it together for more than a few days a week.

At one time I had a trainee nanny from the local college to help me for a few days each week, and my youngest daughter went to a nursery one day a week and a childminder another. I finally had some time to myself but it was getting too complicated and when my mother offered to have the children whilst I worked I immediately said yes. The car I had bought with the insurance money from the burglary gave me a great deal of freedom and with a little money in my pocket I was able to take my mum out shopping on the days I was not working. We helped each other and I felt a lot better.

In time, I found that the antidepressant tablets were holding me back, and I knew I had to stop taking them. The doctor had warned me not to stop taking the tablets in one go but I did it anyway. I literally took the tablets one day and stopped the next. The fog cleared almost immediately and I was fine for a while. I'd missed the psychic experiences even though I feared them and whilst I was taking the tablets I seemed unable to feel the unseen spiritual help and guidance which was my birthright. Guardian angels were with me – but I'd been unable to 'feel' anything when I had been depressed. I lost them, and they lost me.

I still spent a lot of time in front of the television. One day I was watching the daytime television show *This Morning*, which was focusing on angels. It reminded me of the experience I'd had as a child where I'd felt I'd been saved by angels and I began to investigate the whole angel phenomenon in depth. My life suddenly had new meaning. I wanted to find out more about angels.

By this time we had a computer and it gave me the perfect opportunity to learn how to use it. Amazing things were beginning to appear on the internet and at last I was able to do the research that I'd longed to do in the years before. Now I could type any paranormal word into a search engine and the internet would open up the whole world to psychic investigation. It was very exciting.

The week after I'd watched the angel programme my youngest daughter had an upset stomach. I quickly ran out of sheets and towels so I made her up a bed on the bathroom floor and laid her down to sleep on some towels. She called me steadily throughout the day, which was exhausting. After she called me for the twentieth time that day I called out to the universe for 'someone' to come and help me with her as I was now so tired, and again found myself unable to cope.

Much to my confusion, as I walked into the bathroom, the sound of a celestial choir filled the room. I searched the house looking for the source of that sound, and even stuck my head outside the window but I realized that angels (or some other helpful spirits) were showing me they were around and watching over us. Angels were with me, and at last I was able to feel them around me again.

More and more spontaneous paranormal experiences were occurring. Less than a year later I had another 'out-of-body experience' like I'd had as a young child on holiday. I was suffering from a sore throat and was taking antibiotics. One night, and after my husband had gone to bed I decided to get myself a hot chocolate before retiring. As I opened the fridge I spotted the remains of an open bottle of wine in the bottom of the door. I'd opened it a couple of days before. 'Why not?' I thought to myself. This was exactly what I needed to cheer myself up so I decided to pour myself a glass, which I drank quickly before switching off the lights to go to bed. I thought no more about it.

Whether it was the mixture of the wine with the antibiotics, or just tiredness, I was never too sure but as I started to walk upstairs I found myself becoming 'taller and taller'. By the time I reached the top step I was well aware that something was not right. Our house was an older property and our bedroom was part of a new extension. To get the ceiling height in the bedroom, there was a step down into it, so the floor in our bedroom was slightly lower than the other upstairs rooms. As I stood on this top step of the bedroom this particular night, it felt as if the step had been raised somehow.

'What have you done to the step?' I asked John who was drifting off to sleep.

My spiritual body had slipped out of the top of my head somehow, and I was now 'looking down' upon myself in the mirrored wardrobe door. My logical brain was still trying to explain what had happened and I was aggressively questioning my husband, and trying to work out if he'd had someone raise the entire bedroom floor just to trick me! As if! I was standing level with the mirrored wardrobe door yet at the same time I was almost up on the ceiling. How could this be happening?

I took off my jacket and opened the sliding wardrobe door to hang it up on the rail, but instead of my eye line being half way between the two clothes rails as usual, I could now see over the top rail and was amazed to discover dust, which would normally be out of sight!

I figured that my spiritual body had 'slipped' about a head-height above my normal level. All the while this bizarre experience was happening I was actually able to talk in a normal way, explaining what I was experiencing as it happened. How strange is that?

I hung on tightly to the wall as I made my way into the en-suite bathroom but as I walked back into the room my body and spirit had come back into alignment! I was able to see normally. It was over almost as soon as it had happened. I'd had a waking out-of-body experience and then within minutes I had plopped back into my body again. Weird – but also kind of fun!

Over the next few days I told everyone who would listen about what had happened to me and even found someone who'd had the same experience. It wasn't long before I found myself back on the internet and was pleased to discover a lot of websites where people shared their own out-of-body experiences. I found an internet forum and spent many hours talking to other people, before discovering that there were many people who had learnt how to recreate the out-of-body experiences on purpose. This was something I HAD to do! I wanted to do this again and I just had to learn how.

CHAPTER 2

Taking Control

Come to the edge.
We might fall.
Come to the edge.
It's too high!
Come to the edge.
And they came,
and we pushed,
and they flew.

Christopher Logue (1968)

This chapter is where it starts to get a little crazy. Bear in mind I was trying to develop my psychic ability and tune into my angels and the higher realms. I didn't have a clue what I was doing, I just knew that I wanted to do this.

Mostly I was reading about psychic development and out-of-body techniques on the internet and trying them out, which was perhaps not the most sensible thing to have done. The trouble is that at this time, there was no one that I could talk to about these things in my local village. Would you? Can you imagine it? 'What a lovely new dress ... by the way, I am trying to leave my body by a series of meditation techniques ...' You get my point! People would think I was crazy ... perhaps I was, or maybe I still am. I still find it a little hard to share the personal things that I was trying out at that time. But it's important for you to understand who I am.

Although much of what I am telling you might sound a little bizarre, believe me, everything happened exactly as I am explaining it. Through all this time I always felt as if I was being guided in some way. It wasn't just a random series of paranormal experiences, I felt as if I were being guided by a higher source. My angels and guides were with me every step of the way.

'Let Jacky try a little of this, and a little of that,' they seemed to say. With each experience I went out and read about what had happened and what was continuing to happen to me. I explored the subjects and investigated each paranormal experience by chatting to people on the internet. The internet was my lifesaver. And these things just seemed to 'drip' slowly into my life, a bit at a time. In the meantime I was hot on the trail of the out-of-body experience.

Could I learn how to come 'out-of-body' on purpose? Was this the opportunity to begin to control some of the things that had always happened to me? I started asking questions about how other people had experienced out-of-body travel, or astral projection, as it was sometimes called. I realized that for some people there were different types of experiences.

Some websites explained that we have several different spirit bodies – layers of energy bodies, each becoming finer and finer. These faster vibrating bodies enable us to travel to higher spiritual levels. Perhaps, I figured, this is what Jesus was talking about when he said, 'In my father's house are many mansions.' Maybe these different astral planes represented the different mansions. I read about people who'd not just flown about their bedrooms in their spirit body, but had travelled to different heavenly realms and even different planets. I was intrigued and I wanted to do this too. I started to keep a journal of my experiments.

Some people had begun as I had with a spontaneous out-of-body experience (OBE). This might have happened during 'a time of crisis, illness, grief, tiredness or during an accident', I read. Well, I guess I'd been ill before as I was taking medicine at the time of my own first out-of-body experience (although hardly what you could call a serious illness), but I wanted to learn how to do this without being ill just the same. There were many different techniques that people had tried with success. The idea was to get your body as close to sleep as possible but to keep your mind awake. 'This would enable someone to lift out of their physical body…' I read.

Have you ever heard yourself snore? The body appears to paralyse when we dream (a natural phenomenon). The methods of creating both an out-of-body experience and a lucid dreaming state (where we are dreaming but aware that we are dreaming) had similar techniques. I wanted to be able to hear myself snore; to know that I was asleep whilst my brain remained active and aware. This stuff seemed crazy but I wanted to try it so badly.

It sounds unbelievable but these internet people were convinced you could lift your spirit out of your body on purpose. Was this a natural ability which humans had somehow forgotten how to do, or was this 'paranormal'; above and beyond 'normal'? Either way, I was determined to have a go rather than hang around waiting for the next thing to happen to me.

As soon as the girls went to school the next morning, I planned my day. Technique number one involved falling back to sleep with your arms up in the air. How weird was that? As soon as you began to fall asleep your arms would drop and instantly wake you up again. The idea was to get closer and closer to this 'edge of sleep' without losing consciousness completely.

I spent hours doing this technique and eventually was able to reach what some people called 'the vibration stage' (where your whole body ripples as if you were receiving a mild electric shock). It wasn't as unpleasant as it sounds. I was creating some type of psychic phenomenon in my body and I was doing it because I wanted to – I was in control…well, sort of!

Spirits had been visiting me all of my life and now I wanted to visit them and I was hoping that these exercises would help me on my way.

I didn't seem to get very far with the first technique, so I investigated other methods to create an OBE which involved visualization. I was always good at 'seeing' pictures in my mind so I hoped I might do better. With this technique, you kept yourself on the edge of sleep for as long as possible, and then when you felt the 'vibrations' (the shaking/rippling feeling which floods through the body when you are ready to 'project' out of it), you 'imagined' yourself sitting up, standing up, rolling out of your body and so on. Nothing happened. Does this sound crazy? Stay with me here …

Although I wasn't having a lot of success with my training techniques, other strange things were happening to me at this time. Maybe this was related in some way? I felt sure that it was.

One day when I was drifting off to sleep I became 'awake' whilst I was asleep. I was shocked to see something at the end of the bed … it was me! I had achieved the opposite of my goal and lying in bed I was able to see my spiritual self 'stood' at the end of the bed, looking in my direction. To say I was 'freaked out' was an understatement and as I tried to pull myself up in bed, a kind of scream left my mouth. The scream sounded as if it were coming from miles away, a type of echo chamber of some sort. I heard my own voice shout back to me, and as I pulled myself upright the spiritual version of myself flew towards my body at amazing speed and plopped back into place as it had before. I lay on the bed with my heart beating rapidly. Was I excited or terrified? Probably a little of both, but this was just the beginning. Wow!

I gained a little confidence. It was time to try the 'rolling out' of my body technique. I combined it with the more bizarre 'holding my arm up in the air' method and several times I fell asleep, only to be woken up by my hand slapping down across my face. What did I expect?

Each time I found myself getting nearer and nearer to the 'out-of-body experience' and remembered that if I just 'imagined' myself rolling out of bed it would happen. I started to drift off to sleep and within moments was wide awake except my body was paralysed. I couldn't move my physical body but before I could analyse this further I found myself rolling off the edge of the bed and onto the floor where I bounced up and down. I realized I had achieved some sort of success as I properly awoke to find myself still in bed. For a moment at least, my 'spiritual body' had actually left my physical body – or so it seemed. Yet I hadn't travelled to any distant lands, only as far as the bedside cabinet. It was hardly the exciting astral travels I'd been planning.

I was getting desperate. When was I going to start 'flying' to the heavenly realms like others had told me about? It was all so much more difficult than I had thought. I decided to try a different technique and instead of lying down I would sit in an upright chair and meditate. I devotedly sat in this chair and meditated every day for months on end. I was rewarded with more strange experiences.

One day I felt my very 'personality' split into three parts. Each part was 'me' and yet separate. Each 'me' was able to communicate with the other parts and I saw a vision of three overlapping circles. I was in a deep trance when my little dog barked beside me. Someone had posted a leaflet through the door and I came back to reality with a start! Another spiritual journey had ended before it had begun.

Another time I got as far as the 'vibrational' stage again but this time I felt myself lift out of my body. I was aware of floating out of the room, and into the sitting room next door where my husband was watching television. But I had no ability to 'see' where I was going, only 'feel'. I decided to float back to my body and try again but at that moment my husband called out to me to 'put the kettle on'. Instantly I was back in my body and another adventure had ended prematurely. The body is capable of so much more than we realize. We can do so many things but it's as if we have forgotten. Shopping, going to work, watching television ... all these things and more occupy every waking thought. We don't spend enough time exploring other realms, particularly our own inner realm.

I wasn't a mystic or a guru. I hadn't trained for years to create magical states, at least not in this lifetime. I guess what I was doing was weird – and I was unable to share my development with anyone I knew. But still I plodded on with my experiments.

Practice makes perfect as they say and one night John and I had been to a nightclub. We'd had a fun night but as I got into bed my whole body was aching and buzzing with pain. Maybe this was the night to try out the 'exhausted body, mind awake' technique I had read about? People can be so inventive!

As I lay on my side, the last thing that went through my mind was, 'this is a great position to lie in and have an out-of-body experience.' I closed my eyes and lay on my side but within seconds my body began to 'vibrate' violently and I could 'see' the wall to the side of me very clearly, even though the room was pitch black. I realized I was seeing clairvoyantly – with my inner eye or 'third eye'. At last, I was on my way.

I remember thinking, 'This is it, I'm going to have a proper out-of-body experience,' and knew that I'd better not get too excited because it might shove me right back into my body. My heart felt as if it was beating so fast that I might have a heart attack. But everything I'd read about the out-of-body phenomenon suggested that this was the spiritual vibration as the spirit body left the physical body so I worked hard to remain calm.

I found my spiritual self moving rapidly towards the wall before I calmed down enough to think through what was happening. I had made it. Here I was, actually flying free of my body and I had done it on purpose. At last I was having a proper out-of-body experience! Although I couldn't see anyone else, I always felt as if I were not alone. It created a not unpleasant feeling of security, quietly in the background. I was out of my physical body, floating free and totally separate and I had total control of my thoughts and motion. Yes! I could do whatever I wanted.

I began to float towards the end of the bed and, remembering what I had learnt, I directed my movements by using my mind. What should I do? After all this time, I had finally made a conscious exit from my body with full vision and I didn't know where to go and what to do! Perhaps I would float down the stairs? I can honestly say it was all I could think of to do. I could go anywhere and yet I chose to float downstairs!

I whizzed down the stairs in my spirit body at lightening speed. Once I reached the bottom of the stairs I worried that I might forget that this had actually happened. Would I remember that I had done this amazing thing when I woke up again? I began having doubts, and the doubts created a magnetic feeling. Thinking of my body made me automatically draw back to it. I found myself being slowly pulled back up the stairs again, towards where my body lay on the bed. All I could see was a grey blob where my body lay. This was my last chance; could I do anything else before I entered my body? Was this it? After all this time, all I'd managed to do was float down the stairs and then come back again. I decided to do a little twirl before I plopped back into my sleeping body, which instantly woke up again.

I sat up in bed and felt a kind of awe. That had definitely happened – it was real and I spent the next half an hour or so writing up the details in the notebook I kept by the bed. Many years later I started to receive hundreds of accounts from all over the world. Others had done this too and many people, especially children, had memories of floating down the stairs whilst their bodies were asleep in bed. We are so much more than our bodies and after this, I knew for sure.

I did have other travels after that one, but that experience was my favourite and the one where I was the most lucid and aware. Another time I left my body, I floated down the stairs again. It seemed so dark and I automatically leant over to switch on the light before I 'fell' rather ungainly right through the non-physical wall and instantly plopped back into my body once again.

One adventure took me 'flying' through the window and over to a neighbour's house opposite but I felt guilty about entering their house in case they were awake. Would they see me as a ghost? I didn't want to frighten them. This time I flew through the closed window and began making my way down the main street and I lifted higher and higher. I was aware of a sort of breeze blowing past me as I flew. I felt it as if I was actually there ... so I was.

Later that night I woke up suddenly and sat up in bed. I could hear a commotion outside and as I looked out of the bedroom window I noticed a man on my neighbour's lawn. I yelled to my husband to telephone the police and as I watched, another man appeared to be climbing through their front window to gain access to the house. Seconds later, my neighbours came running out of the front door as the two men ran away. The police arrived and disappeared inside the house and I wondered if something about my 'astral flight' might have awoken or disturbed them. I hadn't seen the would be thieves try to break into their house in my out-of-body state after all, and of course I couldn't go and ask them about it! It was just one more mystery and was probably just a 'coincidence'.

On another occasion, I became aware of 'flying' wildly through our local town centre. This time I didn't seem to have any morals at all and took great delight in flying through people's bodies and knocking off the hat of a poor man who was minding his own business and going about his shopping. I enjoyed the idea that no one could see me and wasn't bothered at all about upsetting people. It was very out of character and when I woke up

I wondered why. Had it been real and why had I acted that way? It was dark outside but in my lucid state it had seemed light as before. Had I skipped through a different time zone or was it just a strange and very real dream? Another memory found me flying over rolling hills and when, several years later, I went for a ride in a helicopter it felt strangely familiar as if I had done it before, which of course I had!

Most of my 'trips' were in and around my house. I read several books which explained in more detail how to have experiences in these astral planes and heavenly realms. It all sounded rather unbelievable and I have to admit, without my own experiences I'm not sure I would have believed any of the accounts that people had written about what happened to them! You just get to the point where you go, 'What? No way!' How could this be real? I never had one of these heavenly type experiences spontaneously, although I found myself in a space of 'love' one day. It was totally unexpected.

John and I were having many problems in our personal relationship. We had reached an all-time low, and we had a massive row one night. I grabbed my car keys and walked out of the door with no firm idea where I was going or what I was doing. I sat in the car for a few minutes trying to decide. I wasn't really leaving home, but I needed some space. I drove to the other end of the village where my parents lived and thankfully they didn't ask too many questions. I asked if I could stay the night and Mum made up the spare bed. I had a drink and went right to bed as there was nothing I wanted to say. Mum just whispered that everything would be fine, but I wasn't so sure.

I got into bed and switched off the light. I mulled over what we'd been rowing about and it wasn't even anything important. The whole thing had got out of hand but I wondered if we had reached the end of the line? We never seemed to talk in a normal way and like many parents of young children we didn't go out together as a couple, hardly ate together and just went about our daily routine. Was I still in love? I thought about it for a second and realized that I was. Why was I here? This wasn't where I belonged, it was just normal stress which many people with young children go through.

I imagined God standing before me and I asked him a question. Am I supposed to be with him? What shall I do? I handed over my problem to him completely. 'I don't know what to do, so you decide,' I murmured into the darkness. 'I leave it totally to you to handle.'

I loved my husband very much so I decided to send him some love from my heart over to our house using my mind. I just beamed it over although I had no clear idea of what or why I was doing this. Then my children's faces seemed to appear in front of me so I sent them love too. I had so much love in my life but had forgotten. I thought of my parents and sent them some love and then my sisters and my nieces and nephews. Next my in-laws, and then I tried to remember every friend I'd ever had. Each moment the circle around me grew and grew as I added other family on this side and the next. I imagined love surrounding everyone I knew. I could feel a powerful force growing within me. Love was pouring out of my body in all directions … I was creating the situation for another paranormal experience but had no idea.

Did I love my neighbours? I guess I did, and my whole village and the country and everyone in the country. This image became more and more real as the vision stretched to the whole world and beyond. I visualized love reaching out to everyone. Every moment I felt myself become lighter and lighter and in no time at all I had floated out of my body. I'd done it again but this time it happened on its own.

I became aware of being both in the room and floating in some random space in the universe – or out of it? I wasn't sure. I was surrounded by the most powerful force of love that I had ever felt in my whole life. I was love, I was bliss and I gave in to this love that surrounded me. A strong light surrounded me and the light was also love – the source of the love. I was being held in the arms of our creator and I wanted to stay here forever.

How do you describe something which is impossible to describe? How can I explain what happened to me in any way that will help you to understand what I experienced that night? I had reached out to God and

God had reached back to me. I wanted to stay in the place where he was, to be with him and only him. If I were reading this I would be sure that the author was having a strange dream, or had totally lost it but I honestly hadn't. I had opened up some creative force within me and this force had a power of its own.

Would my children miss me if I didn't come back? I knew they would be fine. Would my husband care if I wasn't here? I knew that life would go on if I didn't exist but that by my not being here and living out my life, many things would change. I had never considered suicide, but being in this place of love felt better than being in my body, which ached with confusion. God had found me and lifted me into his arms and I wanted to stay with him.

I lay in these loving arms of God for the longest time and then I could hear my mother's voice calling me in the distance somewhere.

'Jacky, do you want a cup of tea?' I could hear her calling me in the darkness and I wanted it to stop. If she wakes up my body then I will just drop back into it again like before. 'No, no go away.' I thought, 'I don't want to ever leave this safe place of love.'

I opened my eyes and the room was in darkness. Slowly I sat up in bed and swung my feet over the side and then walked over to the door. 'Yes Mum?' The whole house was in darkness and Mum and Dad were both asleep. The voice of my mother calling me back had only been in my mind … and just part of the experience. Mum had no awareness of what had happened, at least not in any conscious way. Yet later, as before, I discovered other people around the world who had shared similar experiences with me. Other people had felt these loving arms – I was not alone.

The next morning I went home and the girls had both gone to school. They probably didn't know that I had even spent the night away from home. I showered and drove into town, mulling over the most amazing experience that I'd had in my whole life and at the same time, talking to this presence inside of me.

'If you want me to stay and work out my marriage then I need a big sign,' I said.

As I drove over the railway bridge on the way into town I saw my sign. A twenty-foot billboard with nineteen-foot letters was right in front of me, and spelt out the word 'YES'. The advert had been placed there by a car credit company but I had my answer, literally, 'as large as life'.

We struggled on for many years. The biggest difficulty now was that John did not share my spiritual and psychic interests. He would say, 'You're not doing that psychic stuff again are you?' And who could blame him? He must have felt that I was losing my mind, but I was unable to stop the exploration of my inner mind. There was more to life than this and I was determined to find out what it was all about.

We made another trip to my sister-in-law's house in Cardiff and this time it was to celebrate the New Year. I felt tired for much of the time and made my excuses to go to bed during the day. I slept for ages and then decided to try some more meditation techniques. Sitting on the edge of the bed, my mind drifted off to nowhere in particular and then suddenly I began to see a series of images float past my mind like a slide show. Each image came in from the right before floating off to the left. I've heard many clairvoyants say that images came to them in that way and now it was happening to me. Had I opened up the part of the brain which is able to do this?

I had no idea what these images were but it was like looking at a row of Christmas cards. One of the images was a Christmas wreath handing on a red door. I remembered seeing one on a door just like it earlier on in the day. I became aware of someone calling me and it brought my attention back into the room. I was being called down for tea and realized that I had been upstairs for hours on my own. Apparently, they had called me several times but I had no memory of this whatsoever. I must have been a long way away when they called ... at least, a long way away in my spiritual body.

Later in the week I had my first past life memory. My sister-in-law always gave up her bed for us when we stayed over, and she slept in the spare room. It was a big comfortable bed and I had no problem getting off to sleep. I remember dreaming a very boring dream and the colours were dull and uninteresting. Then without warning it changed. Cutting across the dream came a full-colour 'film' with me both as the 'star' of the show and watching from above. I was watching what appeared to be 'me' in a past life, although I certainly didn't look as I do now. I was in the past life and watching it, both at the same time.

My 'dream' had changed into something I had never experienced before. One minute I was having a normal dream and the next I was looking at a brightly-lit stage show. The UK has very dull light compared to the light you see in other parts of Europe and this stark contrast was here in the dream. Below me was a scene of a palace. I was aware of a woman dressed in silks and fine jewellery. This woman was someone I could place in my current life: a family friend whom we always called 'aunt'. Yet visually there was no comparison. The woman in front of me looked nothing like the person I knew today but still I knew it was her.

Kneeing down in front of this woman was a pair of servants – both eunuchs and, rather shockingly, I was one of these. In this past life I was a man, I'd had my male sexual organs removed as part of some secret ritual. I have no idea if this was ever done in real life but in my 'vision', this had been done to me. The person kneeling next to me was almost identical in height and build and a similar appearance but I did not recognize this person from my current life. I was a servant and without my sexual 'equipment' I guess I was safe to look after this grand lady!

As the scene expanded I could see a tall male servant behind my wealthy owner. He had stolen something and I knew that I had taken the blame. I was to be put to death. I had no emotion over the scene, and I just accepted it as it was. I knew immediately that I was being shown a past life of some sort and was both down below, kneeling, and up above watching the scene. I could feel the experience of both watching and experiencing it live at the same time.

As soon as I accepted what I was shown I woke up. The house was in total darkness and silence. I looked at the clock. It was 2 in the morning and I sat up and mulled over what had just happened. 'That was real ...' I whispered into the darkness, and I felt as if it was. I had to write it down, so I made my way to the end of the bed to see if I could find a pen in my bag, but I couldn't even find my bag. I had probably left it downstairs, I figured. I grabbed my dressing gown so that I could go and search for it or at least find a pen. I assumed there would probably be a pen in the kitchen. I had to remember this bizarre vision!

In the morning the 'dream' image of the night before was still clear in my mind. Dreams often fade upon awakening but this just got clearer. As the day went on I remembered more and more of what had happened in this past life. The male servant was also known to me in this life and was another close family friend. He had always cared for me deeply. Had part of his inner being remembered what he had done to me? Had he remembered that he'd had me put to death in a previous life?

This couldn't have been just a dream. For a start, I was already having a normal dream when this vision came into view – it cleared to one side to make room for the past life review. I just knew what I was being shown and it was one more piece of the jigsaw puzzle of my confused life.

This time I felt more comfortable and discussed it with John. To my surprise he didn't doubt what I was saying and just accepted it. We were making progress! I was buzzing all day about what I had seen. This was one of the most exciting things so far. Of course I then began researching past lives and looking at ways in which people had brought past life memories into their current life and why. It was another journey.

Would anyone believe me? Again, as before with my investigations, I found thousands of people around the world who had had experienced similar phenomena, and the larger percentage of the world actually believes in reincarnation already. I didn't try and convince anyone of what had happened to me because strangely it didn't matter what anyone else thought. This was my experience and part of my reality. It was personal to me and that was all that mattered.

If you go looking for psychic experiences, they just seem to happen! Welcome to my world.

CHAPTER 3

Spiritual Growth

We cannot pass our guardian angel's bounds,
resigned or sullen, he will hear our sighs.

Saint Augustine

The previous chapter was a journey through into my spiritual and psychic adventures. I feel that it was necessary in order for me to appreciate and validate the experiences of others. To assist others with their own angel and paranormal adventures I needed to have visited these inner realms myself. To understand my journey was another thing altogether.

The full-time angel investigation was beginning. Are angels a spark of the great divine energy we call 'God'? I wanted to know everything. Quantum physics teaches us that there is no separation between an object and the person that observes it. We and our own consciousness totally affect that which we observe, and I totally wanted to affect my own observations.

I began spending even more time on the internet. It

was the fount of all knowledge as far as I could see, and I realized it was time to create my own website. I wanted to encourage people to write to me about their own angel experiences so I had to try and get my non-technical mind around how to build a website.

John was by now taking a mild interest and supplied all of the technical knowledge except the creative part, which was up to me. I built my first ever website and I was very proud of it. It was cringingly embarrassing and rubbish but I didn't realize how bad it was at the time … it didn't matter. I started inviting people with angel websites of their own to visit mine and before long, I was getting hundreds of e-mails every month.

To start with, people were sharing mainly their own angel stories – we were all looking for some reassurance. Then later, when people started to ask me questions about their own angel experiences, I was able to help. I'd read so many books by this time and of course I'd had so many paranormal experiences.

'This is the first time I have told anyone about my angel experience,' they would say, or 'I told someone about my experience once and they didn't believe me.' I believed them. I'd been there and done that. I was the 'queen of weird' myself.

There had to be a book out there which explained things in a down-to-earth way. I couldn't find what I was looking for. I decided to write my own book about angels and I honestly thought that it would be that easy.

Everyone gave me permission to share their stories and was happy to talk about how they now worked with their own angels. I wanted to put real people's stories into a book. Some people had been through amazing things and other people's stories, although more subtle, were still fascinating.

We were ready to move house. We decided to downsize and sell off many of the inherited furniture we had around us. It was time to clear our clutter and our relationship. Throwing away hundreds of magazines, wardrobes full of old clothes and duplicates of every single kitchen tool was a very therapeutic thing to do.

We filled up one of our downstairs rooms with everything which was too good to throw away. This room had previously been my meditating room and it was now so full you couldn't move in there. A local women's refuge group came with a massive van and took the haul away, including a three-piece suite, armchairs, tables, an old hi-fi, lamps, bedding and curtains.

Clearing the space in our home had a dramatic affect on my depression which still lingered around at this time. Although I was already a lot better, clearing the house made the biggest difference of all. It was now easy to move house – we had whittled down our possessions to half of what we had owned previously so we literally bought a house which was half the size. Throwing and giving things away was amazing. 'Things' have a way of weighing you down.

Moving to our new house created an amazing wave of creative energy. The new place had large, bright windows. Light flooded into the south-facing living room and I began to write. By this time I had hundreds of spiritual books, had experienced so many weird and wonderful things and heard so many fantastic stories. I did feel I was able to help because I could recommend which chapter of which book had similar stories or which book had advice for any particular problem. I could put people with similar stories in touch with each other and was beginning to see patterns between psychic and angel experiences.

My website letters were fast becoming a kind of 'agony aunt' column. I wanted to do something with these letters, whilst I was collecting material for my book. For six months I oversaw the decorators and the carpet fitter and the landscape gardeners. I got away with being at home for six months before John asked me when I was getting a proper job. It was so important for me to write this angel book but I knew it was going to take a lot longer than I had originally thought. Writing the book was my new work.

It was whilst I was struggling for a way to continue doing what I felt I was destined to do that I came up with the idea of writing for magazines. Again, with perhaps a touch of naivety I decided to become a freelance article and feature writer. I paid a visit to my local newsagents and picked up a handful of magazines. Again

I felt I was being guided and brought the magazines home, full of confidence. I poured myself a drink and plucked up the courage to start ringing editors. 'Hello, my name is Jacky Newcomb and I am a freelance writer…' I began. Sometimes not knowing that it is possible to fail is a gift in itself.

The first article quickly followed and others came shortly afterwards. It gave me the experience I needed to earn whilst I learnt, and I had the opportunity to read and study paranormal books for a living. Bliss! It was a massive breakthrough. This is what I should have been doing all of my life. I suddenly understood why I had spent years in a state of depression. With young children, a lot of what you do is a compromise, but now that the girls were older I was able to do more of the things which pleased me. Every day I would e-mail or ring magazines and suggest articles. As soon as an idea was accepted I began the research. I loved reading books about things I was interested in and it was all in the cause of earning money to help the family budget. I continued to collect angel stories and file them away.

I was still getting stacks of e-mails through my website every month and spent many hours answering them. Sometimes I would spend an hour or more answering just one question. There had to be a better way and I wondered if any magazine would take a regular column from me? After posting out months of queries and 'mock up' columns, I finally got my first column, 'Dear Angel Lady', in *It's Fate* magazine.

After quite a while I had written several articles in magazines, newspapers and e-zines (internet magazines) all over the world including, one in my local newspaper, but my biggest postbag, for sure, came from my regular magazine column. I began writing for more mainstream magazines as well as holistic, spiritual and paranormal ones. I often sat down at the keyboard to type and words would just flow from nowhere. Was it from nowhere or was it from my own guardian angels?

I enjoyed reading other people's work on angels and the afterlife and really anything which related to my own experiences. In my column and articles I had the opportunity to promote some of these books which I had enjoyed. I had always spent a lot of money on books but suddenly publishers were sending me books for free. It really helped financially. These items were necessary for research but I would have bought them anyway.

I was walking around the local garden centre one day when I received a telephone call on my mobile phone. It was a publisher asking me if I would be interested in writing a gift book on angels. What an honour! I could barely hear her on the phone. The reception was so poor and Christmas carols were playing in the background. As the telephone rang I was looking at some cherubs on the display – the 'coincidence' hadn't gone unnoticed! The 'gift book' eventually turned into my very large book, *An Angel Treasury*, and even after I had finally finished writing it I had to wait many months for it to reach the shelves.

I lived on a fever pitch of excitement and could hardly believe that this 'baby' was mine. I'd finally done it – the book was complete and I'd like to say that it was the easiest thing I had ever done, but of course it wasn't. The research in its entirety had taken me around seven years to pull together. I had achieved my dream and created the angel book I had always wanted to buy. But the book was so much more than sharing angel stories and suggesting ways that people could work with their own angels; it was a partner to my own spiritual growth. The book and the stories which came with them travelled hand in hand with my own story. It was the catalyst by which I opened up my own spiritual eyes. Life is not a destination, it's a journey and my journey had involved many unusual things along the way. Nothing is ordinary. Every aspect of our lives is learning. Each and every experience is growth.

The book's publication was just the beginning of the journey. For the briefest time after I had finished the book I felt that I had written everything there was to know about angels. What I had written was in fact everything I had discovered so far, but as time went on I realized there was so much more to come! More angel stories poured in from all over the world. Amazing, life-changing and life-saving stories, which needed to be shared.

What is an angel? The answer was different to each person and I felt the need to distribute this information by way of providing the opportunity to read. Being moved by other people's amazing true-life experiences in the way that I had, and sharing those experiences, was part of my destiny.

Hundreds of articles and features in magazines have taken the word into normal homes with normal people. But a second and now a third book were requested. Every day I realize with thanks that I am doing what I love.

When you are ready, read on and be moved, as I was, by the thrilling thing called the afterlife, where angels and our guardian loved ones on the 'other side' watch over us with rapt attention. Love is a greater thing than we experience here in our every day world. We live and feel such a small part of the greater love that is part of the divine architect.

Looking back on that night at my mother's house I remember that feeling of being wrapped in the arms of our loving creator, and it helps me to understand that we are never totally alone. Our guardian angels are with us always, and never more than now have they made themselves known to us.

Part 2

CHAPTER 3

An Angel Saved My Life

Every visible thing in this world is
put in the charge of an angel.

Saint Augustine

Amazing angel stories are being shared all over the world, right now. Our guardians and loved ones on the other-side are sending their love to us every day, and more and more folk are having divine intervention in their lives on a day-to-day basis.

Many people believe that these experiences are 'stepping up' now because the angels are beginning to draw close to us, ready for massive spiritual changes in the world population. There is no doubt that the little pockets of people who are spiritually aware are growing at a massive rate. Even though wars still rage all over the world, there are people who bring hope to these negative spaces.

A single torch in a dark space brings light and hope. Imagine the effect of two torches, or four? Angels are beginning to appear in many people's lives. People who at one time had no belief or interest in these miraculous celestial beings are now beginning to open their hearts to them. Angels bring their messages of hope and affection, spreading the word as they go. Each astounding angel encounter now spreads around the world like ripples on a pond.

Some of these fascinating stories are about our loved ones and angels helping us with simple tasks; sometimes the 'angel' appears to be human, and at other times these stories are extraordinary and even life saving. Most mesmerizing is when an angel experience happens and you are left wondering, 'What was that?' Sometimes if we are lucky, the 'angels' will leave a little symbol or calling card behind. A white feather is a common sign, but sometimes the sign might be a flower, a coin or even a little angel lapel pin!

Angels let us know they are around in a thousand subtle and not so subtle ways. An angel is a majestic being sent from God for our protection and guidance. Angels are pure love and guardians of humankind. Angels don't have their own free will in the way that humans do, and their role is God's bidding. This they do with great devotion.

But we sometimes call humans 'angels' too. When someone has 'been there' for us during our time of need, we say, 'Thank you, you are an angel.' Yet still a few people feel that angels are part of the paranormal or the occult (which simply means 'the unknown'), which in a way they are but really this is because we know so little about them … at the moment. Do not be afraid of this wave of heavenly love! Embrace it!

Angels can perform miraculous life-saving feats as well as bring us comfort and great joy. But angels come in a variety of disguises. Sometimes people write and ask me, 'Can my grandma be my angel?' We will see in a later chapter that although our loved ones in the afterlife are not actually guardian angels they can be there for us in a comforting and supportive role and CAN even save our life on occasion! So they can certainly act as guardians even if they are not actually angels in the traditional sense of the word.

I wanted to explore 'angels' in every sense, including traditional angel experiences, our loved ones in the afterlife, our animals on the other side and even real-life human angels on this side of life. Life, and indeed the afterlife, is full of astonishing and uplifting experiences.

Let's begin our journey with Olivia's story.

Angels Saved a Drowning Man

One summer when I was just fifteen years old, my youth group went to a church camp in Arkansas. On one particularly hot day, our leaders decided to take us to a nearby river to cool off. The first part of the river was very calm and placid, in fact it actually resembled more of a lake, and we spent several hours swimming around. As the afternoon wore on, we discovered that further on down the river was a small waterfall and a deeper area to swim in. It was beautiful and we decided to move down to this area to swim around.

Although the water did not appear to be deep at all, the youngest of our leaders, a twenty-five-year-old man, decided to jump in and see how deep it was. He was a certified diver and we didn't question his swimming ability at all. My best friend and I sat down beside another of our leaders to watch the others and to top up our suntans.

We just sat chatting for a while and then our leader casually mentioned that the man, (who happened to be her little brother), was taking a long time to resurface. When he finally bobbed above water, it became apparent that something was terribly wrong. He seemed to be panicking and really appeared to be in trouble in the water.

He was yelling as loud as he could, but because of the waterfall, we hadn't been able to hear him. We could tell now that the situation was urgent. He was thrashing around and seemed unable to hold himself above the water. It almost looked as though something was pulling him under the water. The group leader became hysterical and we all yelled for someone to do something and none of us knew what to do. We were too far away from anyone else though, so we were left to watch helplessly as this man drowned before our eyes ... it was a nightmare!

By now, we were all out of control; crying and screaming, but my leader suddenly calmed down and asked us to pray for him as that was all we could do. It just seemed hopeless. But, as we opened our eyes from praying, two men appeared out of nowhere and jumped right in. Effortlessly, they swam to the drowning man and easily pulled him to shore. We were astounded! He had obviously been caught in a type of whirlpool, and those two men had managed to swim through it with superhuman strength.

After we made our way over to him, and made sure that our leader was okay, we turned to thank his rescuers, but they had completely disappeared! We were dumbfounded. We searched everywhere for them, but no one else had even seen them.

Later, the man who had almost drowned shared his side of the story. He claimed that when he was underwater he was unable to reach the surface. He said that no matter how hard he kicked he was just dragged down again. He too had begun to pray as he could see no way out of his predicament. He knew that his new wife was standing on the shore watching and did not want her to have to see him die (they had only been married for two months).

No sooner had he begun to pray than his left foot found a rock under the surface so that he was able to gasp a mouthful of air. Then the two men arrived and pulled him out before disappearing as if they had never been there at all!

There were many miracles that day for sure! We really do believe that the two men were angels sent to rescue our leader when no one else could. Thank you God!

This story is amazing and difficult to explain. I guess that these good Samaritans could have just walked away after the accident but it seems unlikely that they walked away unseen by anyone. One thing these angel intervention stories all have in common is that they happen in the 'heat of the moment', when the action happens. Angel experiences are not easy for us to measure in a scientific way, which is why some people find it hard to incorporate them into their belief system. We just can't put an angel story into a test tube or repeat something exactly as it happened the first time ... not yet at any rate.

Belief has to be a matter of faith. Of course if you have an 'unexplainable' experience of your own it helps a lot! I've had many such experiences but I have also read many thousands of accounts which appear 'beyond belief'. These massive miracles seem to be followed by a subtle hint from the angels, which leaves us feeling, 'Is this for real? Did the angels really help us or is this a co-incidence?' We can each only make up our own minds by reading real stories told by real people.

The next story is even more dramatic. Without being accused of using a pun, I would have to say that this story just 'blew me away' and it will you too. How did this family survive this incident? It seems that the angels left a little calling card as angels often do. Here is Noreen and her family's story.

Saved from a Tornado

Cincinnati, Ohio is a thriving, populated city nestled in the heartland of America. Home to major league baseball and football teams, Cincinnati also boasts a renowned symphony orchestra, a ballet troupe and a famed performing arts school. Many consider it one of the major cultural Meccas outside of New York City.

Cincinnati is also right at a point in middle-America where warm air, drawn up from the south seas, tangles with shocking cold air from Canada. The result can be devastating winds that whip into a gyrating cloud of destruction called a tornado. Middle-America is the only place on earth to host this evil weather phenomenon and springtime turbulent weather often produces ripe conditions for a tornado.

But tornados were the last thing on Noreen Bouley's mind as she tucked her two young daughters into bed that night on 8 April 1999. Newly divorced that winter, Noreen had moved the girls to a rental house to start a new life as a single mother. She felt as unsettled as the girls, wondering if she should return to school or continue working as a nurse. It was a relief to fall into bed and allow sleep to black out her worries for a few hours.

Noreen was awakened in the middle of the night by her three-year-old daughter Christina who crawled into bed with her. The clock glared 3.30 am. The late-night invasion was all too common. Noreen worried the girls would never adjust to this different house and life without daddy. Too exhausted to carry her young daughter back to her own bed, Noreen covered her gently and fell back to sleep. It was a fateful decision that may have saved her daughter's life.

At 5.15 am, Noreen jerked awake at the sound of the house shaking violently. Hail pounded on the bathroom skylight, a whopper storm for sure. She gathered Christina into her arms and made her way down the dark hallway to five-year-old Ali's room. She tucked Christina into bed with her sister and suddenly sensed the window was about to blow in. She remembered the instructions at the hospital where she worked as a nurse. Shut the blinds during bad storms in case the glass breaks. Noreen yanked down the blinds and shouted to the girls to hide their bodies under the covers.

At that moment, Noreen felt the window crash in upon her. She wouldn't learn until later that the entire second floor wall was falling in on top of her. The roof rafters cracked above and Noreen sensed the ceiling and roof were now collapsing. She tried to shelter herself under Ali's desk.

'It couldn't have been more than five seconds of total panic and chaos,' Noreen explains. 'Suddenly, I felt myself being swept up and the next thing I knew I was laying on our driveway.'

Slowly, she sat up and saw the girls at the other end of the driveway. 'The odd thing is,' Noreen said. 'the winds in this tornado were clocked at more than two-hundred miles per hour, yet the girls were standing up in the driveway!'

Five-year-old Ali doesn't remember being swept from her bed that terrifying morning. 'I remember there was a storm and Mommy put Christina into bed with me,' Ali said. 'The next thing I knew, I was on the driveway.'

Frightened, young Ali remembers saying out loud, 'What are we going to do?' At that moment, the image of a face appeared. Ali says it was a beautiful, female angel. 'The image was faint, but I immediately felt safe and protected. I knew the angel had saved us,' Ali said.

As Noreen stood, her shoulder was racked with pain. She felt disoriented, as if in a dream. What happened? Why are we in the driveway? A neighbour rushed over to help her comfort the children, and guided them to his house. Ali thought the angel sent the neighbour to help them. Noreen sat in the neighbour's kitchen and thought it seemed very odd. It finally dawned on her that the back wall of his house was no longer there, and she was practically sitting in his yard! 'We've been in a tornado,' he gently told her.

Through all the turmoil, a man transported Noreen and the girls to the hospital where the power was out. Oddly, on that date, the hospital was testing their emergency power to prepare for Y2K. Doctors found Noreen had shattered her shoulder and required stitches on her head and arms. Ali began to vomit, and fearing internal injuries, doctors airlifted her to a children's hospital, where Noreen's ex-husband rushed to be with her. That was when Ali told her father about the angel who had saved them. He was astounded and felt very blessed.

Meanwhile, more angels were at work. Noreen's boyfriend Kurt saw her house on the television news, and immediately remembered the family's dog. He rushed to the scene, but the police would not let him into the house. Kurt left his car, and walked into the neighbourhood where he saw a woman carrying Noreen's dog! The pet was in the laundry room next to the garage when the tornado hit, and evidently escaped unharmed when the garage was totally blown away!

The next day, Noreen was released from the hospital. She did later endure months of physical therapy on her shoulder, but she was amazed the girls had scrapes, but no real injuries. She was awed by Ali's angel. When she returned to her house she was flabbergasted to see the entire upstairs of the house was gone! Even the carpet had ripped away. The only structure left standing upstairs was the bathtub. Water spewed from the burst pipes and the burglar alarm was blaring.

'I had no clothes except for the T-shirt I wore to bed that night,' Noreen said. 'My boyfriend and I climbed in the broken bay window to see the damage. It was a mess. But the kitchen table was shoved into the corner and had trapped a chair. That's where I found my purse intact with my driver's license and some money. There were lots of angels assisting that day.'

Another friend was outside searching for lost treasures. 'My best friend Melissa came up,' Noreen said. 'She held up a guardian angel pin and said she found it in my driveway. She asked if it was mine. I didn't recognize it, but it touched us all. I still have it in my jewellery box.' It seems Ali's angel had left a reminder.

As Noreen continued to survey her house she noticed the stairway was completely collapsed and destroyed. 'I know in my heart, that I would have tried to escape with the girls down those stairs. We got out of that house the only way we could … with the help of an angel. I know we still have an important mission on this earth and I intend to do my best to achieve it.'

Ali has not seen her angel since that incredible morning. But she still feels the comfort that she is never alone.

Our difficulties with belief are often centred around the questions, 'why me?' or 'why would one person be spared when another is not?' It's a complex question to which we don't truly have an answer. I subscribe to the 'It's not your time' theory.

Imagine the power needed to lift someone off their feet. This is exactly what happened to Mrs Ross. Angels? You decide.

Lifted I

It happened during the last war, whilst I was stationed in a Royal Navy Base. I was due on leave a short time later. I intended doing the return trip home via a local railway station, even though I hadn't done so previously.

Once I arrived the only entrance I could find was through two large gates. I walked through but immediately found myself on the train track itself, right in the path of a fast-approaching express train! In the darkness of the night (during the war the lighting was banned for security reasons), I had been unable to see where I was going. There was no way I was going to be able to get out of the way in time.

I uttered a feeble cry for help, not really expecting any, when suddenly I saw a pair of arms, out stretched to lift me. The arms lifted me right up into the air and placed me safely on the nearby platform!

I know that this was done by a spiritual being, which

then immediately vanished. I'm alive to relate all this, just as if it happened yesterday. It was something I will never forget, a miracle in action!

At a recent workshop one of the attendees told me of a 'lifted' incident of her own.

Lifted II

Bernadette says that she has a memory of when she was about eleven or twelve years old. She'd been to the park with her two brothers and her mother. On the way home they had to cross a busy main road. She stepped out onto the road without looking and a car was speeding towards her. She has a memory of being pushed forward out of the way, but has no idea how that can have happened. Over the years she has come to believe that it was her guardian angel that saved her from death that day.

At the time she e-mailed me the story, a couple of days after the workshop, she had a feeling of an angel presence around her whilst she wrote her story. Bernadette has three angels that she talks to every night before going to sleep – Raphael, Michael and Gabriel – and she says she feels truly protected by them.

This next story is strange in that it is almost identical to the two stories above! Are you noticing a pattern here?

Some of these experiences seem to happen over and over again, which appears to indicate the areas in which angels are able to help us in emergencies. Physically lifting someone is one of these ways.

Lifted III

Emma May from England wrote: 'I was just coming back from Birmingham with my aunty and my nanny and I walked out into the road. A huge double-decker lorry was coming very fast at me and I just felt like someone lifted me out of the way. Even my nan and aunty saw me actually in the air and we knew that my angel was with me.'

This is not the end of this particular phenomenon. There is another similar story (Lifted IV) in the chapter called 'Warnings from the Other Side'. The only difference is that Lisa, who was also lifted onto the pavement, knew that the incident happened with the assistance of her own nan, as opposed to an angel.

But for now, let's get back to Mrs Ross again. Her family are not strangers to angel contact and she also explained several other encounters that the family had experienced in the past. I'll let Mrs Ross continue the story.

Peace

Towards the end of the 1914–18 war, my late mother was woken from a deep sleep by what she thought was a rustling of paper, but upon wakening, to her astonishment, she saw two angels present. One carried a parchment scroll, then passed it to the other one to hold. It was then zig-zagged from one corner of the room to the opposite end.

Once this was done, it revealed a message; 'Peace is declared.' And so it was!

In another experience, she explained:

Angels in Church

A Catholic friend came home very excited one day after Mass and her first words were, 'You'll never guess what I saw standing behind the priest!'

The friend explained to Mrs Ross that she'd seen a male angel about seven feet tall, and his size almost took her breath away.

Lastly she recalls:

Directions

Once when my youngest son was hopelessly lost in an unfamiliar place, he was suddenly approached by a young man and woman who immediately pointed him in the right direction (without being asked). Later, my down-to-earth son remarked, 'But they were not of this world!'

This next angel was clearly seen by a whole family, but afterwards seemed to disappear as if into a puff of smoke. Sound familiar again? Was this a real angel or a human angel? Sometimes it is hard to tell the difference but the family knows what they believe.

Angel Saves Son at the Roadside

Julie and her husband, Roger, are the parents of eight children: Sam, twenty-two; Robert, twenty-two; James, twenty; Natalie, eighteen; Alexander, seventeen; Jonathan, fourteen; Stephen, twelve, and Devon, twelve. Four of the children are 'birth children' and four are adopted. The family live in Sale in Manchester, England and are naturally very proud of their family.

When Julie was just thirty-three years old herself, and a young mother, the family went on their family holiday where they parked their caravan in a farmer's field in Devon. The area was a favourite place with the family and they had visited the field many times before.

The field had no gate, only a gap on the hedge that was not visible from the road, but this had never been a problem. The road was a typical Devon lane. It was narrow with high, thick hedgerows, and cars travelled along it at high speed.

It was a hot and sunny August afternoon and the children were playing outside the caravan as they always did, when Julie suddenly looked outside of the caravan window and realized that Jonathan was running away from the rest of the group. Young Jonathan, who was just three at the time, has Down's Syndrome, so his understanding of danger was limited.

Jonathan was running at speed towards the gap in the hedge. At the same time they could clearly hear a car coming down the lane. They ran to catch him but couldn't get to the road in time, and were horrified when they watched Jonathan run through the gap in the hedge in front of them. Julie said it was like 'running through glue' and she knew there was no way that they could catch up with him.

They could clearly hear the car which seemed to be travelling at around forty miles per hour. Julie remembers crying in frustration as there was little chance of the driver seeing Jonathan because he was so small for his age (the size of an eighteen-month-old child).

Julie says they were frantic. They knew the driver could not have seen him and they were convinced he had been run over. But when they got to the road, a man had Jonathan in his arms and handed him over to Julie, saying gently, 'He's fine.'

Julie and Roger were so relieved, but this is where it got really strange. Julie turned to pass Jonathan to her husband Roger and then turned back to the man, but he was nowhere to be seen. Julie looked up and down the lane, wanting to thank him as he had clearly saved Jonathan's life, but he had completely disappeared.

Julie explains, 'Even thinking about it now makes me feel sick, I was so convinced he was going to be hit. It was about 150 yards from the caravan to the gap in the hedges, although it seemed like miles. Jonathan must have been closer to the hedge when he started running because he was playing in the middle of the field with Robert. We were all shouting his name and calling to him to stop but he just thought it was a game.

'Myself, Roger, Natalie and Alexander reached the gap at the same time, which was just seconds after Jonathan got there. The car had sped on past. The man already had hold of him when we got there and we didn't see him pick him up, even though Jonathan had only been there a millisecond.'

Julie says that what was strange was that no one could remember what this stranger had looked like even though the four of them had seen him clearly. None of them were able to describe what he was wearing or anything. 'It was almost as if he didn't exist, and when we looked up and down the lane, although you could see for quite some distance, there was just no sign of him. There literally was nowhere for him to have gone.

'We were both shaking and in tears and we'd never felt so grateful to anyone before. As we were walking back to the caravan afterwards, we were in shock. I was desperate to thank the man, though, and we even got in the car and drove up and down the road to see if we could find him, but he had completely disappeared.'

Strangely, even though the rest of the family felt they had just lived through a complete nightmare, Jonathan seemed completely unaffected by his experience. Even though he was normally frightened by strangers, he was not upset at all whilst being held by this man.

'We've always felt that he had someone looking after him. Over the years, due to him not having a developed sense of danger, he's often got himself into scrapes but he always manages to come out of it unscathed and nonplussed by the experience.

'I'm totally convinced that the man was Jonathan's angel and the whole family knows that something special happened that day.'

Children with special needs seem to carry around exceptional carers from the unseen world. These extraordinary individuals bring joy and compassion into our lives and seem to carry around their own angel guards, as we shall see later.

Cars feature in a lot of the angel stories that people share with me. Our busy roads can be a danger and even though our vehicles are a lifeline for us, many people are in danger because of their vehicles every day. Cars are a hazard! General road conditions; the weather; the ability and attention of other road users; and the roadworthiness of our own and other vehicles all have to be taken into consideration when we venture out for a drive.

Some dangers can be avoided, but others just cannot. Sadly, many animals are also injured and even killed on our roads but these too are a danger to us, as Rob discovered.

Angel Airbag

Forty-eight-year-old Rob Blair was excited as he looked over his new car. The Buick was a second-hand vehicle which had saved him a lot of money. But it was 'new' to him and he proudly pointed out all the amenities to his girlfriend. Air-conditioning, leather seats, even automatic windows.

'It's perfect!' she gushed. 'Let's bless the car.' So right there in the parking lot, Rob and his girlfriend held a little ceremony. They both bowed their heads in a prayer of safe-keeping.

The very next day, Rob decided to spin his new wheels on a drive through rural Michigan in America. It was early autumn, when the luscious forests of upper Michigan brim with deer right before hunting season. Without the hunters, the deer population would explode, but autumn was the season for multiple car/deer accidents.

Rob zoomed along the two-lane highway, the radio blasting, and feeling lucky to be driving such a great car. Suddenly, an eight-point buck leaped from a ditch in front of the Buick. Rob had no time to brake, and crashed head-on into the animal.

'I watched as if in slow motion as this enormous deer with massive antlers hurled over the car hood aiming right for the windshield and me!'

As the deer shattered the windshield, the car's airbag exploded around Rob, a protective cloak of white padding that shifted the animal just enough for the dagger antlers to stab into the seat, inches from Rob.

Rob was astounded to find himself trapped by fur and flesh. Almost immediately a car stopped to help. Amazingly, it was a nurse who called for an ambulance. She had watched the accident unfold before her and was stunned when she found Rob uninjured.

An ambulance and police officer were on the scene within minutes, and Rob felt total protection. It was odd, since not many people travel the rural roads, and what are the chances of a nurse being in the car behind him? He felt blessed.

'The airbag saved me,' he told the police officer. 'Otherwise, those antlers would have pierced my heart and lungs.'

The officer looked confused. 'Where is the airbag?'

Rob checked his car and there was no sign of an airbag. After a careful search, he realized the car wasn't

even equipped with an airbag! 'There is only one explanation,' Rob said. 'I know it was an angel who swept in
and protected me at that moment.' Rob is certain an
angel saved his life.

Many people see a flash of light when they are in a life-
threatening situation and often before impacts of any
type have occurred. Is there a technical explanation
about something happening in the brain, or is this
something spiritual?

Did Frances also see an 'angel airbag' when she was
driving?

White Bonnet

Frances, a fifty-four-year-old carer from Lowestoft, England, was on her way to visit a client. The road was
narrow with cars parked either side, so her main concern was to check for cats, dogs and children appearing
from between the parked cars. Frances says that the
road was so narrow that even keeping between the
parked cars was a challenge.

Driving at less than twenty miles per hour, Frances
was shocked to see another car heading in her direction.

'I saw a huge white bonnet, near my right shoulder,
and knew I was going to be hit. I was only doing twenty
mph, and I think I tried to swerve, but the car hit my
door and pushed me sideways. When I had recovered

from the shock (about fifteen seconds), I turned to look, and the car with the huge white bonnet was in fact small and black.'

Frances was very shaken by the accident.

'I wondered where the white car had gone and the crowd around me were condemning the other driver but I just wanted to console him, because I know he didn't mean to hit me. It was difficult to see and a bit of a blind corner.'

She was unhurt, though, and Frances feels that the angels might have had something to do with it.

'I believe the angels softened the blow for me. I am very grateful for all their help, and thank them every day. I believe in angels, I visit them regularly in meditation. I also talk to them while I am driving. They have always answered my requests for help.'

This was not the first time that Frances has felt angels around her.

The first time I saw an angel was at the birth of my last grandson in 2003. I saw my son and daughter-in-law's guardian angels first and then, when the baby was born, I went to see him in the crib, and his angel was hovering over him. I walked round for the rest of the day with a big grin on my face, and when I relate the tale even now, I still grin!

When ten people at the scene of an incident give evidence they each interpret it in their own unique way. We all see things a little differently. Perhaps it's all just a matter of perspective, after all.

This is another little boy with a powerful guardian angel, but I'll let his mother tell you about the experience herself.

Was His Angel His Mum's Dead Cousin?

A few months ago, my eight-year-old son Cain (who is autistic and has severely delayed development) climbed out of the downstairs window and within seconds he was gone. It was the worst day of my life.

Whilst I was out looking for him, a feeling of complete hopelessness overwhelmed me. Police cars and ambulances sped past at lightning speed and I knew they were going to my son. Imagine my shock when they told me that he had been hit by a freight train …

At that moment, my feelings changed. I can't explain it but I knew he was alive. Once I got closer they explained that Cain had actually been hit by the train which sent him flying through the air, yet for some reason he only sustained a few cuts and bruises.

My son was protected by angels … or was it my cousin who was watching him that day? My cousin had passed over just a few months before the accident. I want to thank them from the bottom of my heart for

letting me keep my son with me. He is my whole life and
I don't know what I would do without him. I'm sure my
son would thank them himself if he could.

The angels already know! Cain would have thanked the
angels in his own way as his 'higher self' would be
aware of the help he received, even if his conscious
mind was not. I can almost see the angel lifting his hat
and taking a bow in the old-fashioned way, saying, 'I'm
just doing my job, m'am'! But perhaps that's just me? I
know that the angels take their role seriously but I feel
sure they also work in great humour when the need
arises, too!

This next story could easily have ended in extreme
tragedy, but Karen was well protected by her regular
angel. Karen is one of many who are aware of their angels being around them on a regular basis. In time I
hope we will all see and feel our angels as clearly as
Karen.

Karen Samuel and I made contact over the internet. I
was amazed when I read about the many encounters
that she'd had with her own guardian angel 'Toyta'. Toyta
is a very 'hands-on' angel and shows his presence directly
to Karen and also through others on her behalf.

Karen went through the most horrific experience at
work one day and her sanity was only saved when her
angel let her know that he was protecting her.

Saved from a Machete Attack

A thirty-six-year-old married mum of two, Karen was working the early shift at her part-time job at her local supermarket store in Middlesex, England. She arrived at her normal time of 7 am and was walking down the stairs, chatting away to a co-worker who was following closely behind.

Karen was looking behind her when she noticed a look of horror suddenly cross her colleague's face. The colleague fled back up the stairs and Karen had barely turned her head to see what had frightened her friend, when she felt a cold hard blade thrust against her throat. From her vantage point on the higher step, Karen's co-worker had spotted the intruder who was wielding a large knife. Karen realized immediately it was too late to run.

'He arrived out of nowhere and grabbed me viciously before shoving a machete against my throat!' says Karen.

Hidden under a balaclava, and wearing a camouflage jacket, the machete-wielding madman made a terrifying sight. Karen thoughts strayed to her husband, Gareth, and their two young children.

What would happen to them, she thought, if I died?

Karen decided to use her family to distract the intruder and asked him not to hurt her, explaining that she had small children at home.

Karen was terrified of the fourteen-inch blade and

was fearful about what might happen to her if she didn't co-operate. She knew that other staff would already be at work. At least forty people worked this same shift and her concerns stretched to her friends and the fear of what might already have happened to them.

Karen and the other staff were unaware, but just two armed men had entered the store with the intention of robbing them of the weekend takings. One of the men had taken the money and made a run for it. The other man had become trapped in the store when the morning shift started arriving for work. None of the staff had any idea who their attackers were or how many armed men were even in the store, so panic was high.

Karen was being thrust further down the stairs by the trapped robber, and by now she could see other colleagues tied up on the floor below her. Almost as soon as she reached the bottom of the stairs he seemed to change his mind.

'I realized straight away he'd decided to go after my friend who was making her escape,' explains Karen.

The madman became crazy and started opening doors to look for her. He dragged Karen to the end of the corridor and shoved her through a door right at the end, all the while shouting and swearing. He knew he had been discovered now and that Karen's colleague had probably run for help.

By a stroke of luck, Karen had been taken into the staff room where other members of staff were hiding. No one dared move for fear of the man coming back. Terrified, Karen slumped into a corner. Her heart was beating madly as she wondered if these were to be her last few moments on earth. But as these thoughts entered her mind, Karen became aware of a presence around her. The presence was familiar to her. Karen had been aware of her guardian angel for a while and says the presence was like an invisible hug. Lights began to twinkle in the air around her and Karen immediately felt safe.

'At that moment, I knew I would be okay and felt safe from physical harm. My angel was with me,' confides Karen.

'A male colleague suddenly appeared from behind some trellis, surprising the robber who tried to run away. My colleague ran off after the madman. I suddenly felt as if a change had begun to happen. The mystical lights disappeared as quickly as they had come and it was then that I noticed two of the canteen assistants had also been hiding in the room. The canteen had a second door which led to a lift. We took the lift right down to the warehouse and just grabbed everyone on the way and ran.'

Many of their colleagues had no idea that the store had been under attack and just chased after the pair of them thinking that there might have been a fire.

Help appeared right after this and as the police began to interview the staff, people began to realize the extent of the madness. Karen's friend had escaped the attacker and just managed to run to the manager's office where she hid under the manager's desk. Unbelievably, the attacker had actually looked in the room but missed her. Although many of the staff had to be taken to hospital suffering from shock, it seems like the angels were looking after all the staff that day.

I was so stunned by Karen's shocking experience that I asked her about how she had originally met the angel whom she felt was with her on that particular day. Karen has had several encounters with her angel Toyta.

Karen had previously worked in a small local shop where she was working next to a pile of boxes which were stacked dangerously. Karen stood, shocked with fear, as the boxes began to topple over her. Other staff could hear her scream out but no one was able to reach her in time.

'I was left standing in the middle of the boxes – not one had touched me! I was so stunned; I could neither speak nor move!'

Karen's work colleagues were desperately trying to dig her out of the boxes and they too were amazed that she was unhurt. Karen felt that an angel must have been watching over her that day but it was when she was ready to cycle home that she realized something unusual had happened. A man, who was walking out of the church opposite the store, walked over to her and placed his hand on her head!

This stranger said to her, 'My dear, do you know you have an angel standing next to you? He's an Asian Indian Prince in a blue silk outfit complete with a ruby on his forehead. He's your very own angel, and he's shrouded in a blue light!'

Karen shivers when she recalls this surreal conversation but even though the whole day had been a strange one, Karen knew that the stranger was passing her confirmation of what she already knew. Toyta her angel prince is always at her side.

Toyta appears to Karen in a very grand way but sometimes our protectors are not really seen at all. They communicate their help in such subtle ways that it is only afterwards that we realize how they must have helped us.

Biddy also wrote to me through my website, and said she felt compelled to share her extraordinary story with me. She too went through the most traumatic and terrifying experience but got through it with her celestial back-up team.

Carjacked

Biddy says, 'I firmly believe in angels and I feel they are very much a part of my life. I am blessed.'

She lives in a suburb outside Johannesburg, South Africa, in an area called Sun Valley, and on the spur of the moment she accompanied an elderly neighbour to the shops about seven kilometres away.

'For some reason I left the house without shoes, jewellery, cell phone, glasses or even a handbag. The strangest thing is that I never go anywhere without any of these items.'

At the time, Biddy never thought twice about that choice although later she mulled it over and over.

'On our way home we were pushed off the road by a car with four occupants,' shudders Biddy.

But the men were armed.

'They jumped out and shot at the ground around the car with a shotgun. We were absolutely terrified. We both tried to jump out of the car and raise our hands in the air to show that we were unarmed. It was one of the most terrifying moments of my life.'

Biddy was on the passenger side of the car but her friend didn't get out of the car quite quickly enough for the assailants, and they dragged her out and started shouting and yelling at her. They roughly forced her ring off her hand and they also climbed into the still running car and stole her cell phone.

Rather bizarrely, Biddy's friend had just taken money out of the cashpoint machine but the money was in her bag which was on the mat behind her chair. They completely missed it.

Biddy says, 'One of the men approached me but wouldn't get any closer than three metres. He kept asking me where my money was. I told him that I had nothing which of course was completely true.'

Biddy then began praying and said, 'Where are these guardian angels when we need them?'

Within seconds the men climbed into their car and sped off at a breakneck speed as if there was something after them. They looked horrified.

'My friend and I looked at each other and were amazed. We couldn't see anyone coming down the road or any sign of anyone, so we had no idea why the men suddenly fled! We jumped into the car and roared off home very shocked at the whole incident. It could have been worse.'

Biddy says that although she was alarmed at the situation, she somehow knew they would be all right. The feeling she had when she looked in these men's eyes was extreme empathy for their plight and their desperation.

'I could feel their pain. Maybe they knew what I was feeling too?'

Later Biddy began to think about why she had left home without any possessions that particular day and what made her leave at all.

'After the incident, my friend said that she would never have coped if she'd had to deal with this alone. We were left with a lot of questions afterwards but one thing is for sure, I know that neither of us were alone that day.'

Although in this story the angels were not physically seen in any way the story is hard to fathom with the facts as we know them. Some people may ask why the angels didn't stop this from happening completely but sometimes they just can't. Their powers are limited to things which are not 'life lessons' or part of our learning path. The angels are not allowed to stop our spiritual growth but there is no reason that they can't lessen the pain as much as possible. We must keep asking the angels to help us and give them permission to get involved.

This next story is from a lovely lady called Alicen Geddes-Ward. Alicen is the author of the book *Faeriecraft* and is married to the talented pagan and visionary artist Neil Geddes-Ward. Her angel also came to her in a time of danger but in this instance, she was not aware that she and her unborn son were actually in any danger at all. Our angels seem to have insight into our future lives and the capacity to guide and protect us in that future when it is not our time, as I said before.

Embraced in the Arms of my Angel

Alicen was heavily pregnant with her son in 2000 and her husband Neil was working away at the time. Alicen was alone in the house except for her four-year-old daughter when she had what she describes as just 'an ordinary dream' which she remembers nothing about now. Whilst she was dreaming though, she remembers being pulled awake and then found herself in a new place and in what she calls a 'new state'.

Alicen explains that she found herself in a place without walls and with no surroundings. The only familiar object was an office desk which she was sitting on.

'A blond man of about my age stood before me and I instantly recognized him. However, I knew that I had never met him before, not in my physical life anyway.'

Alicen felt that the man greeted her as if she was an old and special family friend and she in turn felt this connection between them. Rather strangely, the gentleman appeared to her in a grey business suit and their communication came to her as thought rather than through spoken words. Alicen found herself being embraced in the arms of this kindly man as if her very life depended upon it. She felt herself overwhelmed with a sense of God's divine love.

'The feeling that he had been sent to me was all-encompassing,' says Alicen.

The embrace ended and immediately he was gone. When she awoke she expected to be alone but felt something touching her hand. As she opened her eyes she saw her young daughter had climbed into bed with her and was stroking her fingers so gently. Alicen remembers lying in a blissful state and feeling as if she were still surrounded by her angelic presence. Her daughter was gently sleeping. This special moment contained all that is good in the world ... just for the briefest time.

The next day, as she drove her daughter to kindergarten, she found herself totally distracted by the experience of the night before. Everything around her seemed to hold a magical quality. Fields were glistening with dew and everyone around her seemed to smile. Even the children seemed particularly peaceful.

At first, Alicen did not recognize the man as her guardian angel; in particular he didn't have the large white feathery wings she was expecting! Alicen soon began to realize why her guardian had appeared to her at that time. She had planned to give birth to her son at home but her new consultant realized that there was a problem. She had major placenta praevia, which is normally picked up earlier in the pregnancy. A home birth was now totally out of the question as both Alicen and her unborn son would have been in severe danger.

Alicen's doctors arranged for her to give birth by Caesarean. Her birth canal had been completely blocked so the decision was the correct one. The natural birth would have been fatal for both of them. What a terrible shock!

Months later, she was still mulling over the angelic visitation and wrote the experience down. It had, and still was having, such a profound effect on her life. Alicen says even now, 'I felt as if I had been in the presence of God,' and after the dream she realized that the man who had visited her in such a dramatic way must have been her guardian angel, appearing to her as someone with authority. As Alicen says, 'I took this to mean that my guardian angel will visit me in my work ... and help me in an angelic capacity.'

Alicen says she will never forget the power of her guardian angel and calls upon this energy in times of need.

CHAPTER 5

Answered Prayers

And we can be confident that he will listen to us
whenever we ask him for anything in line with his will.
And if we know he is listening when we make our requests,
we can be sure that he will give us what we ask for.

I John 5:14–15

A number of people have written and told how they felt the need to 'pray' for divine intervention due to an inner 'feeling', and were then rewarded by the angel's assistance (like Olivia's story of the drowning man in the previous chapter). Asking the angels for their help is an important part of working with them. We have to remember to ask angels for their help in our lives and know that it is okay to do so. Angels work for God – they are his intermediaries. Asking angels for their help, as opposed to 'worshipping them', is of course fine.

So many people feel that they are not 'worthy' of being helped by angels or that there are other people who have a greater need, and this is simply not the case.

You have no need to worry; angels love to help us and doing so does not take away their power to help others! Just because we've asked them for several things, we don't 'use up' our angel assistance credit!

You can ask the angels over and over again to help you when you feel the need for support, healing and protection. Ask, and know that they can hear you. Angels are always waiting on the sidelines ready to step in. If we choose to struggle along on our own then they are powerless to help us. Imagine the frustration you would feel if it were you. Actually angels don't carry this emotion but they do feel great compassion for our pain, both physical and emotional.

Remember that just because we can't see them it doesn't mean they aren't there. There are many things in our lives that we cannot actually see, for example the radio waves that surround us and the very air that we breathe. Our eyes aren't aware of everything. Remain open and ready to receive. Angels often have a better way of doing things than we can have even thought of – so be open to alternatives!

Angels can't fix everything because some things that we go through are important lessons for the soul, but they can often lessen the pain and they can certainly play a supporting role by helping us to help ourselves.

A man does not always choose
what his guardian angel intends.

Saint Thomas Aquinas

Do you ever follow your 'instincts'? Always pay attention to this still small voice within as you never know when an angel is calling to you. Angels often bring us information in the form of inspirational thought and those 'light bulb' moments, when it feels as if someone has 'flipped the switch' and illuminated everything.

Sometimes they give us guidance in the form of deep inner knowing. Always take notice of these feelings which can save lives. Prayer is a powerful force and one which research proves is useful in healing. I am interested to find out more about how prayer is tested, but research already suggests that people who are prayed for, even when they are not aware of it, are likely to recover quicker than those that were not.

For where two or three are gathered together
in My name, I am there in the midst of them

Matthew 18:2

Barbara felt drawn to pray for her own daughter, even though she was not immediately aware of the reason.

Angel 'Hands' to the Rescue

Barbara loved her family very much and, like most mothers, worried about her children when they were out of her sight. It doesn't matter how old your children are, my own mother reminds me regularly, you never stop wondering if they are safe!

Barbara was no different from all the other mothers out there. She had a little anxiety over her precious daughter Kathleen who, at age fifteen, she felt was a little too young to date seriously, but just the same, like many girls of her age, she had a boyfriend.

One evening, Barbara was leaving the house to pick up her son Paul from baseball practice. Kathleen asked if she could just go with her boyfriend to pick up his little brother at a friend's house, and she promised to come right back. Barbara felt a little uneasy but Kathleen was not a baby after all so she said yes, and left her with a warning for them to make sure they drove right there and right back again – and to remember to wear her seatbelt! With her mother's words ringing in her ears, Kathleen happily went off with her boyfriend for the short drive.

Barbara recalls that it was a busy day. It was both her father's birthday and also the birthday of her youngest daughter Therese. Therese was already at her grandfather's house, waiting for the family to come over with the cake, which Barbara says she had still to pick up from the store, so as she was leaving to pick up Paul anyway, she decided to drive along the highway rather than the usual shortcut along the back roads so she could collect the cake on the way.

Barbara collected Paul and they raced into the store to pick up the cake and some last-minute goodies ready for the party. But as they got back to the car, Barbara gave a shudder as they heard and saw paramedics, fire trucks, three ambulances and, of course, an accompanying multitude of police cars racing by. It was a frightening sight.

She remembers feeling 'sick to her stomach' and actually said to Paul, 'Somebody needs our prayers, quick.' She wondered if there had been a fire, or even a bad car accident. Little did she know what horrors lay ahead ...

Barbara and Paul loaded the shopping into the car and started their journey. At one of the intersections, Barbara remembers that she had to stop to let more emergency vehicles through, and prayed again, and asked her guardian angel (whom she calls Martha), to go immediately to help the people who she felt were in great need due to the urgent activity of the emergency services rushing by. She called on her angel, 'Those people need you right now, go to them ...' There was a pressing need inside to do this but she didn't know why.

Barbara and Paul called at her parent's house so that they could drop off the food, before calling home to pick up Kathleen so that she could join in the family fun. When they got to the door, Barbara's father suggested that they postpone the party as young Therese had fallen asleep!

'Which way did you go to the school?' her father asked Barbara, before explaining that there had been a bad accident on the back road. 'I heard someone was killed and it happened just about the time you had to pick up Paul at the school.'

Her father had been worried as he knew that normally Barbara would drive that way. He was relieved to see her pull up on the drive as he had picked up a sort of 'gut feeling' that it might have been Barbara involved in the accident. It was strange too how Barbara had felt so concerned for the poor people involved.

The incident was still on Barbara's mind as she and Paul drove the short distance home. As they pulled up outside, the house was in darkness. Kathleen always burned every light. Barbara felt that sick feeling again as she switched off the ignition. Tears fell down her face as she turned to Paul and said, 'It was Kathleen, I know it.'

They both jumped out of the car and ran into the house. Barbara immediately checked the answering machine and breathed a huge relief that no one had called. Kathleen always called her mother 'paranoid' and that's what Barbara was telling herself now ... but her relief was short lived.

Just at that moment, the telephone rang. It was her friend's mother, who worked in the emergency room of the local hospital, and she had bad news. Kathleen's car had been involved in the car accident! All three of them were being transported to the hospital. Barbara and Paul just ran out of the door, not even stopping to make telephone calls to her husband at work or her parents.

As they pulled into the parking lot, one of the paramedics, another family friend, met them at the car with tears streaming down his face. He kept muttering over and over, 'I'm sorry, I'm so sorry.'

The next thing Barbara remembers was talking to the doctor in the hallway of the ER. He asked her if she believed in God, and with that her knees gave way.

The doctor realized he'd not made himself clear and explained, 'No, you don't understand. I mean do you believe in divine intervention?' Barbara said that she did, but was still not sure what he meant. The doctor led her down the hallway to where Kathleen was lying and pointed to her t-shirt. The t-shirt read 'Jesus Saves' and suddenly Barbara realized what he had meant. Kathleen was alive and on a trolley waiting for more x-rays. Barbara and Kathleen fell into each other's arms sobbing uncontrollably. Barbara was so relieved!

Kathleen's boyfriend and his younger brother had also survived the accident and after they were all treated they were able to go home! Staff at the hospital were amazed that they had all made it through the accident with barely a scratch!

Whilst they were on their way home, Kathleen explained to her mother what had happened. She said that it was really weird because, about a quarter of a mile before the accident she remembered her mother's warning about the seatbelt and, knowing that her mother would be cross that she had not clipped it on, she did it immediately.

Moments later, they saw a car coming towards them on the wrong side of the road and as he swerved he hit the passenger side of the car where Kathleen was sitting. The car hit them three times as it spun around in a circle. She says that she felt her boyfriend's little brother's hands on her shoulder, holding her tightly in place, but after it was all over she could still feel those hands, so it must have been something else ... Shockingly, the young boy had actually been thrown out of the back window of the car on the first spin! It was a miracle that he too survived.

The next day they all went to look at the car. The car had been completely split in half, right underneath where Kathleen had been sitting. The car had impacted at over ninety miles an hour, and Kathleen had received the full force of this.

The police report stated that the car door was found fifty feet away from the accident scene with the seat belt still attached. So, when the door broke loose, 'the hands' were the only thing that saved Kathleen's life.

'The Lord knew, long before I did, that my child was in trouble, and I will always praise Him for saving her life and restoring mine,' says Barbara.

Kathleen is now twenty-seven with a child of her own. Barbara recalls the words she spoke just after the accident. 'It was an angel, Mom, I know it!'

Isn't it strange how the family all had a 'feeling' about this incident, almost as if they were picking up some sort of inner knowing relating to the experiences that Kathleen was going through. Is this our angels sending the message or perhaps, in this instance, Kathleen herself who was sending a message from some higher spiritual level? Whose were the loving arms which held Kathleen safely into place? Once again, it was not her time.

This next story features angel teacher Michelle Robertson-Jones, who successfully runs 'Sanctuary of Angels', a safe place for adults and children to come and explore the energies of the Angelic Realm. She empowers all to heal the past and free themselves. This role came about as a result of angel intervention in her life.

Michelle calls her stories her 'once upon a times' and shares her experiences in the hope that they may 'touch your heart and inspire you to seek and find the beauty and light that you truly are'.

She says: 'Through my own journey, I feel I have learned so much, that although at the time it may have felt like a dark and needy time, much learning and light has come out of it. I now know that we all are worthy of unconditional love, happiness, success and prosperity.

I know that we all shine an amazing light, of such beauty and purity, that the universe would not be the same if any of us left before our time. I have also learned that life is a gift and I cherish it as such, even times of roller coaster rides.'

Sanctuary of Angels

As a little girl, fairies, angels and deceased loved ones were part of Michelle's everyday life. As a child she used to enjoy visiting her grandparent's garden and sitting in a fairy ring she had built out of freshly-mown grass. The joy, love and freedom to be herself were all so neatly held in that little girl's fairy ring.

Her bond with spirit and even her very soul she feels soon began to fade as she grew up and the pressures of peers and society meant she had to leave it all behind.

'I left home at sixteen, after experiencing many things a child should not see, hear and certainly feel, and studied nursery nursing. My love for children exceeded my love for anything else.

'At eighteen, I had my own son. I was a single parent living in a mobile home on the seafront. My child was a gift and our days were full of sunshine. His blonde hair, brown eyes and the dimples in his chubby hands were all I needed in my life. I went to work as a children's nanny, and took my little boy with me. Money was always tight, and finding enough to clothe and feed him was a struggle but when we snuggled up tight together every night, nothing else mattered.'

When her son was three, Michelle moved house which meant bigger bills, so she began working in the evenings, as a barmaid in a nightclub. It was while she worked at the club that she met her 'knight in shining armour'.

'It's funny how you just meet people and know what role in your life they are here to play. A sparkle in the eyes which stirs a memory, so faded, and not completely clear, but you align perfectly together and you know the meeting is not a coincidence.'

They got married a year later. Michelle arranged for her little boy to have his own ring so the three of them could be united together one day in May.

'I cried as I left my son for the first real time, to venture off on our honeymoon. It didn't feel as if I was going to be away from him for a few days; it was more like we would not be together in the same way again. I did not have the reasons why I felt that way, something was just brewing, that wobbly feeling, in the pit of your stomach that comes before a storm.'

Exactly a week later, life began to change and the hard life lessons had begun. Michelle had discovered she was pregnant and the pair visited the hospital for the scan of their first child together. Something had gone terribly wrong.

'No one could say exactly what the matter was, which meant a trip to King's College Hospital in London where the equipment was more specialized. We were devastated when we found out our baby boy had a chromosome deviancy, a syndrome that rarely affects the unborn, but it had found our baby.

'At the time I was so angry I could not even cry at his funeral. I held it all in, missing him inside me so much. I had no baby and no pram to push.'

A year later Michelle was taken into hospital again; this time with an ectopic pregnancy. Michelle says that she carried 'another soul, not quite ready to face the world'. She found comfort in her angels and asked for their help. The pain of losing another child was so great.

Finally, in March 1997, a perfect baby boy was born six weeks early, with hair all black and sticking up, and oh, so beautiful.

After that she seemed to be 'constantly pregnant'. In 1998, another baby boy was born, seven weeks early. Into the world he appeared, so tiny but ready to fight the planets and prove he knew how it was all done. And then in 1999, another ray of pure sunshine appeared. A little girl was born with hair the colour of chestnuts and a feisty spirit. Michelle believes that her prayers were finally being answered and angels were certainly watching over the family.

'How blessed we all were. The house full of tiny miracles everyday, the first smile, new words, first steps, riding a bike without stabilizers, with a grin you'd pay money for. Goals being achieved, as the four of them, began to grow into beautiful flowers.'

Then Michelle's health began to fail.

'I discovered I was pregnant again but this time I was told that I was too poorly to keep the baby. I was devastated. More illness followed. I became more and more ill and one day whilst I sat in the hospital I began to write to my husband and children, the words on the paper full of love, but not an ounce of feeling in my heart. I couldn't allow myself to feel, I had to go. I just could not cope any more.'

Michelle's life had been so up and down she needed some help from the heavens and the heavens responded.

'The most incredible thing then happened in that room, an experience that no words can ever express, a beauty of love and purity that I could not begin to describe. Then sparkly, white lights, began to surround me, like thousands and thousands of heavenly stars, the brightest light imaginable, but not harsh to the eyes. And this "light" poured pure love and incredible strength over me, enveloping me in a mixture of emotions. I immediately began to feel better. An enormous strength came with the light. The words I had written on the paper, the pain, hurt and anger started to disappear. But I cried. I sobbed till my body shook, that cold, heartless exterior completely melting, in what I can only describe as "Heavenly Energy".'

The little girl inside Michelle opened up to the angelic assistance and she was ready to face the world again. She began to explore many holistic subjects including healing and all this time the sparkles of light were still around her.

'Three major operations later, with a diploma in holistics, a marriage that appeared to have been dragged through a bush backwards and much, much soul searching, things came together again. I then took some angel workshops, and the angels truly, truly flew back into my life, with trumpets, confetti of all colours and white feathers galore! I had found what I was looking for. The sparkles now change colour so that I even know which angel is with me!'

Michelle feels that she has found her life in the angels and now works with them full time. She sees the experiences she went through as lessons and believes that she has grown from them.

'I am only human; I am not saying I am perfect. I still have much learning to do, which is an exciting adventure. But now in those cloudy days, I listen, I really listen and find the rainbows hidden amongst the cloud's lining. Lessons do not have to be as great as mine and many others, if only we listen and open our hearts, first to ourselves and secondly to the beauty of life around us.

'In the past year I have been able to receive messages from the angels and I have learnt to trust more. I channel angel energy for healing, and now hear messages of love, guidance and wisdom to give to others. I know and trust that I was saved to see my children grow up and to help others, so that their lives may also be filled with love and joy from the angels.'

Michelle's story is a beautiful one of lessons learnt and angelic help and guidance. Many people's lives are changed forever when they have been touched by angels, although not everyone decides to go into the 'angel business'; many people follow a holistic or spiritual path after they have had angel experiences. I know – this is what happened to me. Angels change the way we think of the world and it is hard to imagine life without them being a part of it. Even Michelle's powerful 'love' experience sounded exactly like what I experienced myself.

Encountering an angel makes you feel different and gives you an awareness of another time and place. How could one fear anything, knowing that these awesome beings were around? Their abilities seem endless and as mere humans the totality of their role is beyond our understanding. All we have is the entirety of our experience and those of others. We have so much more to learn. The angels are letting us in on their unbelievable power a lit-tle bit at a time. What can an angel do? Anything at all.

This next story is about a lady who was terrified of flying. Like many people who are frightened of flying she felt sure that the plane would crash just because she was on it. She vowed never to fly ... that was until the opportunity for a fantastic holiday in America tempted her, as it would have any one of us.

Everything was going well, right up until they reached the airport. Even then, it was fine at first. She seemed to be coping until they had a two-hour delay in Detroit due to storms. There was no way she wanted to fly in a storm! The plane seemed to sit on the runway for ages and rocked frighteningly in the high winds. The pilot jokingly suggested that although storms were on their way, he would have a go at taking off if the next plane made it in okay! Shortly afterwards, the plane did indeed take off.

In less than twenty minutes she found herself in the grip of the nightmare she'd always feared. Lightning flashed through the air outside of the plane, and terror gripped her.

My Blue Angel

The crew strapped themselves in as the plane was being tossed around and you can imagine that by now I was almost hysterical with terror. The plane was being thrust around the sky. Even the crew were unable to leave their seats as the plane was thrown about. I could see my worst nightmare coming true. A large scream was beginning to rise in my throat!

Just then a blue haze started to appear before me; I couldn't believe it. Right in front of me appeared a beautiful blue angel, complete with white feathered wings. I was just stunned.

I could feel the angel lean towards me, wrapping his wings around my shoulders in a protective sort of way. The scream just died away before it had begun.

Had anyone else seen the angel? I looked around but it soon seemed obvious that no one could see the angel but me. Then the angel spoke, 'Do not be afraid. I am holding the plane.'

I couldn't believe it. The angel just vanished into thin air. I felt totally calm and serene. The angel appearance was all I needed. What a wonderful experience.

I wish that I could say that this was the end of the story but the plane was still being thrown around and I soon started to panic again. After a while the angel came back, and as before I felt calmed … for a while! As the plane continued to shake and rock around dangerously I could feel myself becoming alarmed again and as before, the angel appeared before me again.

This time he appeared with his full strength and said to me, 'You will not fall. I am holding the plane.' I could feel his inner emotions and he was asking me to just be

calm and trust that he was doing his job. I knew we were
being looked after and I was never again afraid of flying.

Angels are nothing like the cherubs we see on Christmas cards. They are awe-inspiring, breathtaking,
majestic beings with fantastic powers. Angels work in a
time and space outside of our understanding but it
doesn't mean that miracles don't and can't happen. Humans constantly compare such things to our own
abilities. Some say, 'Angels can't exist, they are just a
fairy tale.' We cannot imagine how something so unlike
our own existence could be out there.

I used to laugh when I saw those programmes about
other planets. We humans felt that life could not exist
unless there was a ready supply of water and heat on the
planet and yet we haven't even discovered everything
that lives on our own planet yet.

In quite recent history we discovered life at the bottom of the deepest seas, where pressure and lack of light
would kill any human. Not all life needs the same things
that we do ourselves. As a race we can be so arrogant
about such things. We still see ourselves as kings of the
castle, or leaders of the pack.

I find it easier to take my logical brain out of the picture. Even if we did have the ability to fathom the
angels' powers, I doubt that our human brains could
comprehend their greatness, so let's just enjoy the ride –
literally! Proof, if it were ever needed comes in the form

of thousands – probably millions – of real life angel stories from every part of the globe.

Julie feels angels are around her and her family and even believes that angels saved her own children's lives. Here is Julie's story. Remember the white light we talked about earlier? Here it is again.

How Many Miracles Do I Deserve?

Kyle was born very quickly on 20 July, 2000, at 11.00 am in Worcester Ronkswood Hospital and as a consequence, we were placed in one of the side rooms off the main ward. 'Coincidentally', my sister had had her little girl two days earlier (even though our due dates were six weeks apart!). It was great to be able to hobble a few yards down the corridor to visit her!

At around 9 pm that evening I began to settle for the night. Kyle's father Brian was about to leave when he decided to change Kyle's nappy before he left. Within seconds of lying Kyle on the bed he turned blue and went rigid. Brian threw him over his shoulder and raced into the corridor shouting for help. By the time I'd hobbled into the corridor Kyle was already at the end of the ward being resuscitated. I was just horrified. We had no idea what was happening.

After ten minutes and no joy, Brian and I were in floods of inconsolable tears, but during these agonizing minutes my sister experienced a light at the end of her bed. She'd been dozing with the curtains drawn around her cubicle and became aware of panic on the ward. The light was very bright and at first she was afraid of it (especially being very sceptical about the afterlife). She was actually fearful that the light had come to collect her daughter.

Afterwards, my sister explained that she had felt pinned to the bed and unable to move. After a few seconds she felt at ease because the light seemed to emanate a feeling of great love and she felt that the light was connected to our father who had died very unexpectedly in the very same hospital two years earlier.

Eventually they managed to resuscitate Kyle but the signs were not good. My son was placed in the special care unit, and we were informed by the doctors that we would not be leaving with him. We were just overcome with grief but would not give up hope. Something had appeared to my sister that night and we tried to console ourselves that it was a sign.

After a few days the doctors were astonished that he seemed to be beating all the odds. I was told he would probably stay in a vegetative state due to the lack of oxygen to his brain in those few minutes but I just didn't believe it – I knew that my baby would be okay. And he was.

Kyle is now a gorgeous lively three-and-a-half-year-old boy. He does have a medical condition, but with daily medication he's fine. I've since met the doctor who resuscitated him that day and she told me she couldn't understand why she felt an urge to continue the resuscitation. The usual time, she told me was six minutes. She said that after ten minutes she believed my son would be totally disabled and felt very sorry for me, but still she continued.

Unbelievably, Kyle's diagnosis highlighted a problem that his older brother Jack also has (but in a milder form). Because of this incident, the problem has now been dealt with much earlier than would have been usual.

How many miracles here? I'm so blessed!

This story had a double blessing. This terrifying incident could quite literally have saved Jack's life too! It did strike me as strange that the white light initially indicated a fear of a passing over to the other side, which just goes to show how our culture has integrated the phenomenon. Of course, as we will see time and time again, these lights more often indicate the presence of the angels, and not necessarily that they are here to take someone to the afterlife!

Ask for angels to create magic and love in your life – ask them to bring helpful people into your existence and steer you in the right direction. And mainly ask them for their support. You are never alone. Here is another amazing story.

Protected by Angels

On 18 November, my daughter was in a terrible accident. I was running late and I wanted to get home from my friend's house to show my daughter our new puppy, but as I was driving down the road to our home, she passed me on her way to work (she had just started a new job and it was only her second day).

Sheila still had eight months left at college and as I passed her I thought to myself that she seemed so small. I carried on driving home and decided to call my mother-in-law who'd been feeling ill, to see if she needed any help. I promised to send my husband, Jay, to the store for her. I told Jay what she wanted and he started to leave when the phone rang. It was his mother telling him to take an alternative route as there was a bad accident near our home.

Jay ran the errand and returned, but was stopped by a police officer in the driveway. The bad accident was my daughter Sheila. She'd been hit broadside by a truck. I could tell that the police officer was very pale and I couldn't even speak. As you can imagine, we were totally shocked but immediately in my mind, I begged God to take me instead, not my tiny feisty daughter who had just started to live.

Sheila was flown to a trauma centre which was a two-hour drive away from us. It was the longest drive I ever had and my heart sunk lower and lower, the closer we got to the hospital. We were met by a social worker who took us to her.

Amazingly, she had survived the initial shock and was going into emergency surgery. She had a broken hip and pelvic fractures as well as a punctured lung and broken ribs. All I thought was, 'Thank you God for sending the angels to look after her.'

After several days, Jay went to take care of what remained of the car. He said he felt sick just looking at it, even as a well-seasoned Marine. He forced himself to look into the car for her books and things and there lying on the seat (what was left of it), was the angel pin I had give her the year she graduated ...

I had made plans for her to go to Paris as her graduation gift. After 11 September I was worried and doubted whether I should let her go, but it was a sad time and I so wanted her to see something beautiful in her life. At the time my friend was selling angel pins so I bought one for her to keep with her on her trip. It had been with her ever since.

Her car was crushed beyond recognition but I believe she was not alone. Many times during her recovery she would talk in her mind to a friend from school called Jessie. She would tell me all about Jessie's visits but in the ICU it was family members only, so I couldn't understand who she was talking to.

Several weeks later when she was feeling a little better I asked her again who Jessie was. Although we didn't realize at the time, Jessie had died two weeks before Sheila's accident. Jessie had already passed to the light but came back to watch over Sheila in her time of need. We know that Jessie is an angel now and I believe in angels and miracles.

I send angels to everyone who needs help now, and we often think of Jessie and say thank you.

CHAPTER 6

Mini Miracles and Brief Encounters

There are only two ways to live your life.
One is as though nothing is a miracle. The
other is as though everything is a miracle.

Albert Einstein

Miracles need not be earth-shattering events; sometimes miracles can be small things which happen in our
lives … small things which make a BIG difference.

Sometimes angels pop in and out of our lives like a
whirlwind. They jump in, give us the help, guidance and
warning that we need and then go. It happens so fast we
are left wondering, 'Did that really happen?'

Do angels speak? Well, in theory no, at least not in a
language that we would understand, but there are many
cases where people have heard voices either in their
head or as a physical voice. Sometimes it is difficult to
tell the difference. Angels communicate in thoughts and

ideas – whole concepts of information will occur to us in one go. This transference of information is a more natural way of communicating for angels.

Having said that, there are occasions when people will hear an isolated voice bringing an urgent message from an angel or spiritual guide. If the information is needed quickly, then a voice is what we will hear. Sometimes it's just a single word or a short phrase like STOP, or SLOW DOWN.

Edna-Mae didn't mind either way – she knew that her guardians had spoken and she listened. Her daughter Jill shares the story.

Salve

Many years ago, back when my dad had to travel a lot for his job, he came down with a strange rash. A doctor examined him and couldn't really determine the cause, but said he had seen people who had caught scabies from hotel rooms. He suggested that my dad use a strong salve in case this was the problem. He also said my mother would have to use it too because the scabies would spread on the bed sheets.

That night, my mother slathered the salve all over her body as the doctor prescribed. In the middle of the night she awoke. Her chest felt heavy and she had to struggle to breathe. Suddenly, she heard a loud voice shout, 'Get that stuff off you NOW!'

Mom leaped out of bed and jumped in the shower still wearing her nightgown and scrubbed off the salve. She felt poorly for the rest of the night, and later found out the salve contained a toxic pesticide that could have killed her!

Luckily, her husband was fine, and suffered no reaction.

I remember hearing that 'angel voice' once myself when I was driving to my sister's house (I told the full story in *An Angel Treasury*). As I was about to drive over a local Bailey bridge (a single track bridge with traffic lights at either end) I heard a loud warning voice which shouted, 'Pull over to the side!'

After arguing with the voice and having the warning repeated a couple more times I finally pulled right over to the side of the road, scraping up against the hedge. But it was just in time because a large white van came over the bridge and clipped the wing mirror of my car with such a loud bang it made my heart beat very fast indeed. If the warning hadn't come, the van would have hit me head on!

It's hard to imagine that a voice would appear out of thin air. You'd think it would be scary, but actually it wasn't for me – just urgent. I felt that I had no choice but to follow the instruction and others have felt the same. These guardian voices help and protect us with utmost urgency – and thank goodness that they do!

Tracey from New Zealand listened too …

Stop!

It was late, around 10 pm, and I was alone in the car. I remember I was driving home after visiting some friends. We drive on the left hand side in New Zealand and I had stopped at a red traffic light, indicating to turn right into the major T intersection with no indication of the danger that lay ahead.

I was in that lovely, almost meditative state you can get into when driving home from a pleasant evening. We all do it and even though I was relaxed I was still aware of the road and in control of the car. I was waiting for the lights to change, and as the traffic light switched to green, I put the car into gear and went to drive through the intersection as it was now my right of way.

Suddenly, a strong voice shouted 'NO!' The voice was so urgent and powerful I immediately obeyed. I just sat at the lights and I didn't, and couldn't, move forward, and it's a good job that I obeyed the voice! As if from nowhere, a car flew through the intersection on my right, running straight through the red light! I was startled to say the least.

Shock ran through my mind as I realized what might have been. Had I ignored my angel I would have been severely injured or killed.

You know, the funny thing is that I wasn't particularly surprised. Hearing voices is certainly not an everyday experience for me, but I've always felt there is more to life than what we can see or scientifically prove. Being protected so wonderfully was a truly beautiful experience for me.

This happened many years ago now but I can still feel the calm and peace which washed over me at the time. It wasn't my time to die and my Angel made sure I was safe.

The messages are usually very brief. To manifest the voice in this way seems to take some serious effort on the part of the angels! So even more reason to pay attention!

My friend Jill e-mailed this powerful and mind-boggling story.

Disappeared!

I was on my website reading the community forum and I was amazed at this story.

A woman was describing how many amazing things have happened to her. She was driving along a curvy road and her friend was in the passenger seat. She explained that when they were going around a bend in the road her passenger suddenly started screaming because a pick-up truck was in the wrong lane and barrelling towards them.

It was very scary because she said she had no time to move out of his path. Can you imagine how terrifying that was? All she could do was shut her eyes and wait for the truck to hit them. I couldn't believe it when she said that the crash never happened, and when she opened her eyes again, she could see the pick-up truck in her rear-view mirror and back in the other lane as if nothing had happened.

Her passenger actually saw the pick-up truck disappear right when it should have hit them and then reappear in the correct lane immediately afterwards. Both ladies felt that their guardians had saved them that day as I do.

Shona, from the UK, had a frightening experience in her car and she too experienced a strange, unexplainable phenomenon. Notice here again that white light and the perfect help arriving from nowhere, which are now both familiar to our angel stories.

Pushed

A year ago I was travelling by road to Cornwall with my husband. We usually stopped a couple of times during each trip as I always suffer from travel sickness, but this time we had to make a third stop because I had a terrible feeling come over me! I had a drink of water before we continued our journey along the motorway.

Almost immediately we saw a large animal in front of us. I'm not sure what it was but it was already dead in the road. There was nothing I could do to avoid it and as I hit it, I completely lost control of the car and went right over a bank at the side of the road at a speed of around 70mph.

I immediately cried out for help and as I did so, I saw a white burst of light and my life flash right in front of my eyes. The next thing I remember was coming to in the stationary car. We had overturned in a ditch at the bottom of the bank! My husband was fine and didn't have a scratch on him. At first I thought I was stuck inside the car but an invisible energy pushed me gently forward and allowed me to climb out of the wreckage!

When I looked down I noticed that I had a gash down my arm, even though I couldn't feel any pain at all. Two men appeared from nowhere and did first aid on me to stop the bleeding, and afterwards I only needed a few stitches!

I believe this light and energy was divine intervention from the angels as there is no other way to describe how and why we are still alive today!

Another friend, TV presenter and author of the book *Past Life Angels*, Jenny Smedley, told me about her own angels. The deep feelings of emotion that Jenny describes are similar to feelings I have had myself so I can really relate to what happened to Jenny here. Once again the feelings of the most amazing LOVE. Jenny shares her story in her own words.

Angels Supporting Me

I suppose I started to get a two-way connection with 'somebody up there' the very first time I appeared on TV. It was in Belfast on a late-night chat show called *Kelly*. I had never been on television before in my life, and I was terrified. I wasn't a good flyer, so I was already unsettled by the flight when I got there, and I knew that Belfast audiences were renowned for being tough. I was going to be on 'live', with the show going out as we made it, so there was no room for error.

I was shown into the green room and they told me I was the last guest, top of the bill, as it were, which only added to my terror. The green room at UTV overlooked the studio area and the producer pointed out the floodlit chair down below, saying, 'You'll be sitting there.' There was a live audience too! I was starting to think that I'd have to make a bolt for it. A live audience, a live performance and a subject (past lives) which, while dear to me, was a well-known foil for comedy! What on earth was I doing there?

I went through the procedure; make-up, wardrobe (my chosen outfit blended so well with the background that I would have appeared as a bodiless head, so they had to lend me a jacket!), and then I found myself standing in the wings, looking across the cable-strewn floor of the set. I could see the audience members peering over the scenery to see who was coming on next. I can honestly say that if my publisher wasn't standing right behind me, blocking my escape route, I would have done a runner right then and there. I looked across at the 'hot seat' I was about to occupy, and knew for a certainty that I was going to freeze. No way could I walk across that gap.

I heard the commercial break announced and received a nudge from behind. The very next thing I knew, I was sitting, surrounded by giant BBC-type cameras, the audience a blur behind them, facing a total stranger across a desk – Kelly. I had no recollection of propelling myself there. The commercial break ended, the questions began, and the answers … just came, from nowhere. I know I was being helped from an unseen source.

Later that year I was travelling to Norwich from Somerset, to take part in a Christian-based programme called *Sunday Morning*. Given that I'd done several TV shows by then, talking about my past life experience, I knew enough to be aware that this was going to be a tricky one.

I was with a friend and I told her that I wanted some quiet time to meditate. I knew that I was being put 'up against' a regular presenter on the show, a vicar's wife, who was going to argue that reincarnation would never be accepted by Christianity, and so I knew I was going to need some help.

I went into one of the deepest trances I'd ever experienced. I could literally feel my vibration increasing, leaving the train far behind in another reality. I could still hear the sound of the train in a peripheral sort of way, but it really didn't exist in the same plane as me, and if it had suddenly caught fire I could well have been impervious to the knowledge.

All of a sudden I found myself in a presence. At the time I had no idea what it was. I had an impression of vast golden light towering above me. I had an overwhelming tidal surge wash over me, a love so deep that it transcended human love by a magnitude. This love was given and reciprocated on an equal footing. It's very hard to describe the whole gamut of emotion and feelings that flooded through me. It can only be understood when it's experienced. It is overwhelming, and makes it very clear in a second, that all we know and hold dear of this physical world is as unimportant in reality as a grain of dust in the vastness of the Universe. The feeling was almost like a dog and master, in terms of devotion, but with absolutely NO subservience at all. The love and the obligation was given and received in total equality. I felt divine, and yet at the same time I was like a child wanting to please a parent. Not because I felt I had to or out of duty, but because pleasing the parent would fill me with joy and double my own happiness.

I was shown a scenario by this being; it contained three paths: one central path and two smaller ones running parallel with it. The side paths were my first book, and my connection to my past life soul. The central path showed a person (who could have been me) being given the role of 'seed planter'. This person would set seeds in people, while sharing her story with millions all over America. I was shown that this person would be attacked at times, maybe even physically, and might eventually have to live in a protected environment. The 'being' paused, while I considered what I was patently being offered.

Instinctively, without any hesitation at all, I said, 'Let me! Let me!' I was desperate and determined to be given the task of seed planter. I would have done whatever I had been asked. Making this being happy was the very same thing that would make me happy. The 'being' agreed. It was simple, but it was binding. I only found out later that I had 'made a contract with an angel'.

Needless to say, when it came to the interview, the answers, as always, were there. I was placed firmly on my pathway, and I've been on it ever since. Every time things seem to slow down, a new tool emerges, and off I go again! Like I said, knowing why you're here and walking with purpose in the direction you know unshakably is right, is essential to well-being.

Nowadays I sometimes get answers to questions that haven't been asked, while I'm meditating, and I have the certain knowledge that the question WILL be asked someday, and that I will be ready with the answer to it when it does.

So, I'd found my role, my aim in life. I became a des-
ignated 'seed-planter', passing spiritual messages to
incarnated souls. I did not have to exclusively plant the
seed of reincarnation and karma, but ANY tiny seed of
awareness. Awareness that the material world we struggle in is not the be all and end all some people think it is.
That there are more important things to worry about
than having the best car, best house; best furniture that
some people concentrate their whole lives on. That real
violence is not glamorous, but is dirty and horrendous.
That on the day we die, we will need spiritual prosperity
and that being the wealthiest person on the planet in
terms of money will mean absolutely nothing at all, and
do nothing to help us.

Having this purpose in life overrides everything; hope,
fear – everything. It's something I can always come back
to and ground myself with, as is that angelic visitation.
Just to remember the power of the love-force I felt, is
enough to bring me back to my centre.

Also, of course, I'd had the fear of death removed
which is something that is guaranteed to change anyone's life! So afterwards I pondered on the 'contract'
I'd made and wondered how it could be possible for
one person to share their story with millions of Americans. We feel the need to ask 'how?' Well of course
now I know 'how'. I would imagine that speaking on
350 or more radio stations across the USA would
reach millions of people, and of course by now I've

written dozens of articles for on-line and print magazines too.

It's not all easy though. It amazes me how challenged some people feel when confronted with someone who believes in reincarnation. However, thus far I have not been attacked physically ...

A lot of people tell me I'm brave to have 'stood up to be counted'. I don't see that at all. Bravery is being afraid and still acting, but in my case I had no fear at all; I was compelled to speak up, so bravery didn't come into it.

A lot of people also call me 'lucky'. I don't see that either. We make our own luck by watching for signs and following them, by raising our vibration with meditation and asking for what we want. It amazes me that people can't be bothered to do that. It must be very frustrating for angels who are trying to communicate, but just can't slow their vibration down enough to get through.

They ARE there; just ask. Once you understand the path they want you to walk, then it makes sense that they are going to help you succeed. Another important thing is to show willing. Once you think you know what you're meant to do – take a tiny baby step in that direction, and if you are right – doors will open.

Jenny is a very spiritual lady and very open about working with angels. I remember when I first started writing about them myself and how hard it was to open myself

up to ridicule from others. Even recently, whilst walking through my local shopping centre, someone I used
to work with spotted me and called out, 'Hello fairy!'
Luckily, a sense of humour helps a lot!

One of the most difficult talks I have done was for a
charity fundraiser at my local rugby club. It was frightening to stand up and talk about 'working with my
angels' in front of my home crowd (although they were
very kind)!

Following your path and following your belief system
is important. Happily, as time goes on, this particular path
gets easier for me to walk! Yesterday, I had just finished
checking over the manuscript for my book *A Little Angel
Love* which had been sent over, beautifully laid out by the
publishers. I decided to pop round to my mother's house
and show her all the little angel details in the book, because I was so excited. Even though she is literally five
minutes' walk away I nearly always take the car because I
am usually so busy. Just as I was about to get the keys out
of my bag I changed my mind and decided to walk.

It was a lovely sunny day and I felt good as I crossed
the road and carried my angel book manuscript securely
under my arm. Then something caught my eye. A perfect white feather floated by at eye level and as I turned I
watched it fly off into the distance. What great timing! I
certainly felt the angels with me that day! Angels support our every step, so step bravely in the direction of
your choice.

Janet feels she is surrounded by kind angels who help her out with all manner of tasks, each and every one, a 'mini miracle' in itself. This story has the urgent voice again.

Simple Tasks

In October 2000 I saw an advert for a fantastic trip to Canada, which was run by a local firm. The company picked you up from your home and brought you back again which would have saved on paying for London hotels, and lots of travel arrangements. At the time, my mum-in-law was living with us so we decided it was not possible for us to leave her, and sadly by the end of October the trip was fully booked.

During December we heard that a flat was available for Mum in a home where she could have nursing care if needed. We were thrilled for her but this also meant that now we would have the freedom to take the trip if we wanted to. Although it was a long shot, my husband visited the travel agent to see if there were any cancellations, but as we suspected it was just too late.

One day in January I came home from work and I again thought about the holiday. 'Perhaps,' I mused, 'I will ring the travel agent tomorrow,' but an inner voice told me to telephone NOW.

The manager seemed surprised at my call and said, 'Wait a minute, some places have just become available for seats not booked in Glasgow. You are a very lucky lady.' I had to pay there and then with my credit card as all the places would have gone in half an hour. So, Mum settled into her new home in January, and we had a marvellous holiday in Ontario that Easter. Thank you, Guardian Angel.

Another time I was 'down in the dumps' a bit, and asked for a sign that I was doing useful work for the Holy Spirit. Two days later, while cleaning the house, a voice told me, 'There is an angel here,' and I turned to see the most glorious golden 'being' in the corner near my kitchen door. I was on my knees cleaning the hearth anyway so I just put my hands together and said thank you to God.

Angels have helped in other small ways too. Although it sounds such an insignificant thing, I kept getting the same craft book out of my local library and said jokingly to the librarian, 'If ever you have a sale, this book has my name on it.'

I tried everywhere to get a copy but couldn't as it was out of print. A book search company wanted to charge me £62.00 for their efforts. In August 2001, we went to Hereford on holiday and visited Hay on Wye. Hay has the most second-hand book shops in the UK and having searched lots of shops and feeling hot and tired, I asked my Guardian Angel to help me find the book. Within seconds it was in my hands and even better, it only cost me £2.95. I realize what a lucky person I am.

No task is too small. Remember that if it is important to you then it is important to the angels. Does your request interfere with an important lesson in your life? If not then the chances are that they can help. Life is not about suffering but love. So I'll remind you again – always ask the angels if they can help you!

If you want to call on specific angels for help then you certainly can. I once ran an article for a magazine, about asking the Archangel Chamuel for help in finding lost items. It was hysterical when the letters started pouring in from people who had tried the exercise and had been successful with the technique. This letter was from Jean.

Bank Card

I lost my bank card the other day and after looking all over for it, I decided to ask the angels to help me find it. I must add I have a little angel altar in my bedroom which I use very often and this very day I went up to the altar to do my meditation and I could not believe it. When I moved a candle to light it, there was my bank card right underneath.

Here is another one from a lady called Helen:

Papers

My boyfriend lost an important paper with a PIN number on it that he needed. We searched the house high and low and gave up hope until reading your advice to call on Archangel Chamuel.

I repeated the request for two days, then when I was awoken by what sounded like a rustling of papers, I rechecked a drawer and there was the missing paper on top! We were amazed.

Since then we've experienced coincidences. Songs have played on the radio at appropriate times, items have fallen off supermarket shelves as I've walked past and last week the car in front of ours had my initials on its number plate.

Thank you for your advice on finding lost objects and the difference it has made to my life.

And lastly this one from Mrs Jenkins:

The Lost Necklace

My daughter had lost her necklace. I had bought it as a present for her last year. For two weeks I searched the house and looked in every nook and cranny. I went through every drawer and every cupboard – twice. I thoroughly searched the house.

When I went shopping I picked up my magazine and read your article and decided to ask the angels for their help as you had suggested. I didn't believe it would turn up but the next morning I went to a drawer to get something and there it was. I never moved anything, it was just there.

I asked my daughter Geraldine when she came home from school if she knew where it was, and she was so shocked as we both had that drawer out three times and knew it wasn't there, so where did it come from? I will never doubt the angels again. I know it was the angels that brought the necklace back.

When I sat and thought about it, I remembered that I had asked the angels back in September to free me from pain. I have suffered with back pain for over ten years. I hadn't immediately realized but I decorated the whole house from top to bottom in six weeks and never had time to think about my pain. It was only when my husband mentioned that I wasn't taking my pain killers every day or rubbing creams and lotions on my skin that I remembered. The angels had taken my pain away too.

Mrs Recardo asked her angels to give her some simple proof that they were around her. This just goes to show how industrious angels can be.

Feather

I believe we all have our own guardian angel but I had never thought to ask for proof. After reading of the experiences on your website, I decided to do just that. I lay on my bed in the evening, thinking about what you had written, and I asked my angel if she could hear me to show me a white feather.

Nothing happened at once but when I went to kiss my daughter goodnight, I found her face down in her pillow tugging at something poking in her face. It turned out to be the quill end of a feather which she pulled out with her teeth and gave to me. I told her what I had just asked for and we had a good laugh.

I still had a few doubts though, so the next day whilst I was picking up my mail I asked for further proof. On opening a letter, I gazed in amazement at the picture of an angel on the front of the catalogue inside. I certainly believe in angels now and get great comfort from knowing they are around.

It's a special miracle to meet your angel face to face. Angels often show themselves in dreams as they regularly do to me. Wendy has seen her angel.

Angel in My Dreams

I have met him in my dreams. He is tall, broad and African. He appears when I need comforting or reassuring. He gives me a hug or holds my hand, although he doesn't talk to me and I don't see his face clearly.

Sarah's angel helps her with money, although my angels told me to earn it myself!

Banking Angels

In the past three months I have won money on Lotto scratch cards. It always happens when I have only £20 left in the bank and one to two weeks before I get paid. Today I won £35 and I was so happy. In April I won £37 and in May I won £12 and £14.

I never ask for too much, just enough to see me through. I always say thank you when I win and I believe someone is watching over me, checking I am okay.

A few times I have felt someone touch my shoulder as I lie in bed trying to sleep. I have my own thoughts about who it might be!

Well, you never know. I guess it is always worth a try.

CHAPTER 7

Our Loving Animal 'Angels'

Until one has loved an animal,
a part of one's soul remains unawakened.

Anatole France

Have you ever had an animal which made a real difference in your life? Often our pets make a big impression in this life and even the next. I remember one day my cat jumped up onto the bed and circled round and round until she snuggled up and went to sleep. Another time I felt her jump up and 'pad' the bedclothes as cats tend to do. Nothing unusual you might say ... except that the cat had long since passed over to the other side! It seemed a natural and even a comforting thing to have happened at the time, and it wasn't in the least bit frightening.

A dear family dog used to be felt by many family members long after she passed. Suzie seemed to have set up residence at my parents' house (where she'd lived) in the hallway. I swear that when we went to visit my parents, we could all feel her brush up against us and hear her wag her tail! This seemed to go on for several years after her passing.

My friend Wendy once had a visit from a little dog which ran in the cat flap, through the kitchen and then run right out the front door. The dog looked suspiciously like the dog which had belonged to the previous owner, but of course, the little dog was a spirit!

Why do these animals continue to visit us after they have crossed over to the other side? Love is strong and there seems a natural attraction to stay with those you love. Love seems to cross all spiritual boundaries! Sue wrote and told me the story of her German Shepherd Daisha.

Still Here

Daisha was fourteen years old when she died. It was just four years ago when we had to have her put down and I was devastated. She was 'my' dog and she was always by my side as I got on with my daily tasks. She would even sleep on my side of the bedroom floor at night.

Daisha and I had a strong bond even though we were her third owners. She came to us when she was five years old. A couple of evenings after she had been put down my partner Dave and I were sitting watching television when we heard the noise that Daisha used to make when she lay up against the front door and scratched herself. It was so real and it lasted for ages. We even heard the door being gently knocked to and fro and this was a unique sound that only she produced.

As I stood up to check the source of the sound it stopped instantly, but we both definitely heard it. Since then I have felt her walking right beside me when I have been out in the dark and alone. It's as if she is still with me and protecting me.

We have an American Bulldog now who is absolutely gorgeous. I hope we have the same strong bond.

My friend Martine sent me this story of a family pet who made it safely to heaven. If the love is there, then the contact is possible.

The Dog Is Safe in Heaven

In October 2000, I visited one of my aunts, whom I had not seen for seventeen years, shortly before her husband's death. Although my uncle was also my godfather, I did not attend the funeral as I had just given birth to my second child. We had a lovely time together and did loads of reminiscing.

Back home in Leicester I went to see a friend, Wilhelmina, who was a psychic. As soon as she opened the door, she told me that I had brought a visitor from the spirit world, and she proceeded to describe my uncle in his naval uniform, an exact match to the photograph I had seen in my aunt's lounge! He was happy and passing on the message that I was doing a good job.

On another occasion, Wilhelmina told me that I was in the company of two ladies. As she described them I recognized both my grandmothers. They were younger than when they died and my maternal grandmother was dressed as she was when she was in her twenties. However, I was quite puzzled when Wilhelmina said that my paternal grandmother was holding a little black dog (a poodle). I did not give it any more thought and I was just glad to know that they were happy and that I had their love and support.

In September 2001, I paid a visit to another aunt, my father's sister whom I had not seen for a good long time. We talked a lot about angels and unusual experiences. When I mentioned what Wilhelmina had seen, she started crying and then explained that the previous year her dog, a black poodle, had died in her arms after a painful illness, and she had asked God to let her mother look after her. After the initial shock, my aunt felt greatly comforted.

I have formed a strong bond with many of my own pets. Cats in particular have a special place in my heart. Wendy had the same connection with her own cat.

George

For many years we had a black and white cat called George. He was a real character, a true member of the family. George lived to a great age for a feline; he was eighteen when he passed away. I would like to think that George had a happy life with us in our little village. He had a rough start to his life as he was abandoned as a kitten and rescued by the wonderful people at the RSPCA. We became his owners when we chose him to become our family pet. He was about three years old.

About three years ago, just two days before Christmas, George suddenly went off his legs. It happened very suddenly; one day he was fine and ambling around in our back garden, surveying 'his territory', and the next he sauntered in on four very wobbly paws and had to sit down every few steps. He resembled a little old man that was very out of breath.

Obviously, I was very concerned and immediately called the vet. The vet took a long and thorough look at George and I could tell by her expression that there was very little hope for George's recovery. It broke our hearts, but we made the decision to have George put to sleep, to let him die with dignity, with the family that loved him so very much all around him. I held him in my arms while the vet gave him the injection that would give him peace and eternal sleep.

For about three months after Christmas that year, we looked out of our kitchen window to the little grave in our garden that we have brought George home to. It seemed only right somehow to make his final resting place under his favourite shrub in the garden. We swore that we would never have another cat. No cat could ever replace George. Each time I went into the kitchen to wash up, the bowl of water caught my tears as I looked out of the window.

At Easter time that year, there was an advertisement in the local paper; 'Homes for unwanted cats and kittens'. Still with heavy hearts, we went along to have a look!

Enough said. Within minutes we had seen her, a beautiful black and white cat, about three years of age, who was so timid that we had to coax her out of the cage with a tasty treat. It took a few weeks of tender loving care, once we got her home, to convince our beautiful black and white feline friend that we meant her no harm and that she had come to a home that would not abandon her in a carrier bag, full of kittens, as had happened at her previous residence.

When 'Chloe' had been with us for about eight months, Christmas time came around again, the anniversary of George's death. Although we loved our new cat to bits, obviously we thought of George often as the two cats were as different as chalk and cheese. Chloe was a livewire that now settled into her home, and brought us 'gifts' on a regular basis: frogs, birds, butter-flies, even daffodil bulbs. If she could carry it in her mouth, she brought it for us!

One night as we were all sitting on the settee watching TV, Chloe suddenly leapt up off my knee, making me jump, as I had no idea what had disturbed her. She continued to fluff herself up into a giant furball and started to growl and 'swear' at something, like cats do when they're in a fight.

By this time we were all most perturbed as none of us could see anything that she could possibly be growling at. I followed Chloe into the kitchen where she sat and growled angrily at the catflap in the back door. Suddenly the catflap slammed shut, although there was nobody near it. Immediately Chloe sat back down, brought down her spiky heckles and turned around to walk back into the living room. I am convinced that Chloe could see the spirit of George in the kitchen, possibly near to her pot of prized meat, and that is what had made her so very angry!

Since that night, whenever it has got around the time of George's death, our security light will suddenly go on and the cat flap will rattle. I suppose a cynic would blame the wind blowing or a leaf scurrying across the patio, but I know what we think, our little old man comes back for a visit, says hello, sends love and then saunters off again.

There are any number of stories of our pets coming back to say hello from the other side. Do they know they have passed over? In most cases I would say yes, but the love between the pet and the owner keeps them coming back in the same way that it does with our family and friends. Sometimes our visitors are just attracted to a loving home.

Animals seem to be able to see things that we cannot pick up with our normal human vision. We accept as a fact that dogs have a wider hearing range. There are even special dog whistles, whose shrill sound is perfect for a dog but unheard by our less sensitive ears. Our pets' vision seems to be the same! Maybe they can see the spirits of animals and humans alike. There certainly doesn't seem to be any lack of stories on this phenomenon.

I heard about this next case when the owners wrote to me through one of my magazine columns. Lynzi and Lee share their story.

The Visitor

My husband and I moved into a small bungalow a few years ago with our two cats, Kevin, a black Persian and Frankie. When we felt a cat jump on our bed one night not long after we'd moved in, we thought one had snuck into the room when we closed the house up. However, there was no sign of a cat, except for a purr and a dent in the duvet. When we put our hand over the dent, it felt cold and we realized we had a spirit cat.

We named this new family member Spook, and over time, we began to notice her more regularly. We even began to see her sometimes. She is quite a big cat and grey in colour. Sadly, the following summer Kevin died and we were devastated. You can imagine how delighted we were when we realized our remaining cat had noticed that there were now two spirit cats. They have a tendency to tease poor Frankie at dinner time. We can't put his food out in the open because they sneak up on either side of him!

In 2002 I found out I was pregnant and we faced a terrible dilemma. The bungalow was tiny. There was no room for a baby, but we were loath to move because we didn't want to abandon Kevin and Spook. Fortunately, I have a friend who taught me a meditation so that I could speak to them and ask them to move with us. We weren't sure if they had until I spotted Spook sitting by the patio door of our new home (Kevin was always a shy cat, so we see him a lot less frequently).

Now our baby is almost ten months old and loves to play with all three cats, and either Kevin or Spook has taken to sitting on our chest of drawers and throwing things at my husband when he enters the room!

I thought that this would make anybody who has lost a pet smile, and give them a little hope that they will see their pets again.

I'm sure she's right. Our pets can also teach us so much – both on this side and on the other. My own cat Tigger seems to have such great joy for life and has certainly given my old dog Lady a new lease of life. I love to see the two of them chasing each other around, or even snuggling up together.

We searched for him after I started to have many dreams about a new cat coming into our family life. I quite clearly dreamed of a ginger tom cat. My husband was not keen but after my younger daughter Georgina also had a similar dream, John went along with the 'common vote'. Georgina actually said to me, 'Mum, the kitten will be ginger and I have dreamed of him playing with a butterfly.'

Tigger was one of three kittens we went to see and he was the bravest of the three, although still frightened when we picked him up from the home of his carer, a volunteer from the local cat protection league. We brought him home in his travel basket and as I carried him up the drive I saw my first butterfly of the season so I had a little private smile to myself. Was this the butterfly Georgina had seen in her dream? Perhaps it was a clue to the time of year we were bringing him home, or maybe the butterfly was an indication of the fact that he was to be our little angel? Many people see butterflies as an indication of the presence of spirit, and angels also use this method of announcing their presence.

He is a gentle and sweet cat and is certainly an angel to our family. The dreams indicated that it was time for him to come to us, I'm sure. There was just no way I could ignore these compelling thoughts and I just had to go out and find him. It makes you realize that so many things in our lives are planned in advance! I laugh every morning when he bounds up the stairs and jumps onto the bed. He almost has a smile on his face which seems to say, 'Hello, it's me!' I always want to reply, 'Yes, I know, I remember you.'

No, heaven will not ever Heaven be;
Unless my cats are there to welcome me.

Anonymous

Dogs are very sensitive to human emotions too and seem to sense when we are in danger. Their caring nature and love of their owners can often lead to dramatic life-saving situations like this one.

Dog Rescues a Child

A few years ago, Karen noticed bizarre behaviour in her pet. Her dog, Sally, who was previously very well behaved, suddenly began trying to go upstairs and pull her owner with her. Although confused and slightly annoyed with her pet, who seemed to be desperately trying to pull her out of her armchair, she decided to pay attention.

When it became obvious the dog wouldn't rest until she went upstairs, the woman followed and decided to check on her children just in case her pet was picking up on something which she herself had not. Karen was amazed when she entered the bedroom. One of her children had had a major fit of some kind, and was lying face down in a pool of vomit. If it hadn't been for the dog, the child could easily have died.

Dogs are sometimes trained to warn their owners of oncoming epileptic fits. They seem to be able to pick up on the electrical changes within our body. A natural ability to our pets which seems supernatural to us!

Dogs often use their own natural instincts to protect and care – or are they sometimes prompted by our angel guardians to do these things? Perhaps it's a little of both. I read an article today about a baby who'd had a lucky escape and survived thanks to the natural instincts of a dog. The story took place in Kenya, where children playing heard the sound of a baby crying. The baby had been found by their own dog whilst playing around in the nearby woodlands.

The pet gently carried the baby in its mouth and lifted it across a busy road and even through a barbed-wire fence. The dog had tenderly placed the newborn in with its own puppies so that it could care for her.

When the owners found the baby, they took it immediately to the hospital where it was treated for a fever as a result of having been left out in the open. The young baby was lucky to be found by the dog. The nurses of course called the baby girl Angel!

I had a great e-mail today. I thought you might enjoy this lady's experience.

The Perfect Animal Carers

I have a day-care centre and today one of the moms was rather worried and discouraged about finding work and was anxious about her financial situation. I suggested she visualize good things happening for her. Then I told her about the angels and explained to her that she should ask them for help. I told her they are all around us and just waiting to be asked. I guess I was quite animated, as she said, 'You sure have beautiful blue eyes.' I like to share the good news with everyone.

In two weeks I am going to visit my daughter in New York. I had just heard from the 'house and animal care person' that he was unable to come and look after my pets, and another friend, couldn't do the whole week either.

As the children and I were heading outside, I remembered the angels and said, 'Angels please send me someone good to housesit, who will look after my animals as I would myself.'

As soon as we got outside I thought about my friend Dave who owns some rentals behind my place. I remembered that another friend and I once talked about 'house sitters' as she was in need too. She mentioned she was going to ask Dave's daughter Jen, and that got me thinking. Well I started walking through the yard and I could hear Dave's voice. I have a very large yard and I couldn't see his vehicle over the fence. But I went, and sure enough, there he was with his daughter's sports car, below the fence.

I started chatting, telling him about my New York trip which was in exactly two weeks, and his daughter Jen came out and started chatting. I wondered if I should ask her and I just felt myself asking. She said yes! In the fall she had gone to Costa Rica for three months and rented out her place. So now she is just staying with family and friends till she gets her place back. It was the ideal solution for us both.

My cat jumped up on the fence, (one of my four I was afraid to tell her!). She said, 'My mom has four cats.' After we talked they got in their car and drove away. It was perfect timing. Thank you, angels.

My animals are very precious to me and it's very important to get the right people to care for them and I know that Jen will be great.

Remember to ask angels to take care of your pets in exactly the same way that you would ask them to take care of your other loved ones! The angels will be only too happy to oblige.

Now let's go back to some more animal angels. Dolphins have long been associated with their abilities to heal humans. For many people, that 'once in a lifetime' event in their lives often includes swimming with dolphins as a goal. And what an amazing experience this can be.

Marine animals (cetacea like dolphins and whales) send and receive sound signals which affect the human DNA, according to research being done at the Sirius Institute in Hawaii. Using natural biotechnology, dolphins may heal those humans who swim with or near them using sonar. The institute explains that the dolphins and whales are highly intelligent, self-aware beings that use sonic 'tools' to transmit information. Dolphins have a complex language which includes over a trillion words. The Sirius Institute believes that these cetacea are even more intelligent than humans and are working hard for their legal rights to be recognized. Most cetacea have brains larger than ours (up to six times larger in the case of the sperm whale).

There are many stories which indicate that dolphins are able to communicate using telepathic-type contact. Children in particular, have been shown to respond to the dolphins in a way that they have never responded to anything or anyone before. The dolphins seem to understand the problems and illnesses we have and may be picking up signals from our own energy field.

At a local alternative health exhibition recently a lady took me to one side and told me about her own tragic story. Many years ago her daughter and her granddaughter's lives had been taken by her son-in-law. Her own life was still under threat and she and her remaining granddaughter (whom I was lucky enough to meet) were currently under police protection. It was a harrowing story, but she told me about a holiday that the two of them had shared. A local fisherman was kind enough to take her young granddaughter out in a fishing boat and dolphins had come right up to the boat. One had come so close that her granddaughter had been able to stroke the dolphin. The local fisherman had well understood the ways of the dolphins and suggested that the dolphin had sensed that healing had been needed.

I believe that angels are now coming to Earth as animal angels with a mission. Let's face it; we need all the help we can get at the moment. These animal angels are using their higher consciousness to communicate wider issues, and bring comfort and joy to the human race, as well as teaching and even life saving as we have seen.

These higher-level intelligences are communicating through the bodies of cats, dogs and horses. Some people report amazing spiritual connections with parrots and other birds, and for those lucky enough to have contact with wild breeds, dolphins, elephants, lions and tigers too. Certain types of ape have also shown their higher selves to their human owners.

Recent research around the world has indicated much higher intelligence in many of these animals than was previously thought. Even their natural selves are capable of so much more than we give them credit for. The whole planet is evolving at a faster rate and animals are a part of that.

Working with these animals in our lifetime (caring for and loving them) helps us to open ourselves to a higher consciousness which ultimately helps us to evolve spiritually. In this way we see animals as angels who help to create spiritual growth whilst at the same time growing and evolving themselves. The oversoul of the animal is working from a higher place and often through higher level evolved beings. It is not necessary to believe or even understand this – just feel it.

'We can judge the heart of a man by his treatment of animals,' said Immanuel Kant. So our treatment and respect of these creatures is paramount for our own evolution.

Angels are working with our pets, wild animals, human souls who have passed over and even natural elements like the oceans, woods and forests and other green spaces. People feel the angel energy in many outdoor spaces and reach that 'God space' within themselves at the beach, or during a stroll by the local fishpond. It has never been easier to touch the celestial realms and work with these higher energies. Our pets are just one more piece of the puzzle.

Sometimes spirits use birds and animals to communicate with us after a loved one has passed away. Robins, blackbirds and hummingbirds, a wide variety of butter-flies (particularly those with unusual colours) and animals including dogs, cats and horses amongst others appear to us as messengers from the afterlife. Nothing can take away the pain of losing a loved one but maybe this friendly robin eased Angela's grief just a little. Here's her story:

The Friendly Robin

My son Colin died on 19 October 2000, just two days after his 18th birthday, from sudden adult death syndrome. I have had a fear of birds ever since I was very young but for some reason I am not afraid of my new visitor …

A few months ago as I was walking through the park a robin came and sat very close to me. Every day for weeks afterwards this same robin came to me and something inside me told me I had nothing to fear from him. I felt the robin was different in a way I can't de-scribe. I found myself looking out for my little friend every day on my morning walks.

I was asked about robins again just today. Sam was very worried about her father who has been seriously ill. She wrote:

The Brave Robin

While I was away at the weekend with my dad, we were in the gardens at the Chalice Well Gardens at Glastonbury, England. We went down to this tree at the bottom of the garden and I remember it was all twisty and really lovely. We were discussing what kind of tree it might be and my dad reached over and touched one of the branches. At the same moment he was holding it, a robin jumped down and perched right in front of his hand. It just sat there looking at us. I told Dad it was there and he moved his hand in closer and closer and the robin didn't move at all; he was practically touching it when it casually hopped onto another branch.

Dad suggested that I should have a go and I did the same thing, moving my hand towards it until I couldn't get any closer, and it didn't mind at all. It was strange. As soon as it hopped down I felt afraid that it could be an omen – I knew something about robins and my aunt has had messages from people crossing over in this form before.

It was preying on my mind and when I got home I tried to look up the robin and all I could find was that it was a bad omen if it came into the house.

Anyway, this morning on my way to work, I was stuck in a traffic jam so I was twenty minutes late. As I was nearing work a song came on the radio about being time to go and as I pulled into the car park a robin flew down and sat by the car. I stayed in the car watching it as the song finished and then it flew up into a tree and sat there quite happily with me looking at it before it finally went away.

As I was walking into work I said out loud, 'I don't know what the robins mean …' and then I found a white feather down at my feet.

Robins, and many garden birds, become very friendly if they are in a place where humans regularly feed them. Having said all of that, I do believe that birds are used by spirit as messengers but it could well be that the spiritual relatives of your loved ones are gathering around or bringing healing of some sort, so do not panic if a bird keeps tapping on your window or hangs around the house – its nesting spot could be close by. As before with the white light, it doesn't necessarily mean that the angels are coming to take a loved one away.

I suggested to Sam that she keep a record of the appearances to see if she could find any patterns emerging with this or any other appearances.

Sheena's dad communicated in a variety of ways after he passed over. She was also visited by a rather annoying magpie too and she wondered if the two were connected! Magpies can be annoying anyway so it's difficult to tell. She e-mailed me her story.

The Annoying Magpie

Jacky, I cannot explain why, since last week, I have been pursued by a scrawny-looking magpie! I know it sounds really funny and everyone in the family is teasing me over this. This bird scared the life out of me as I was not too keen on it being around, but it seems quite tame as it will fly over and take food from me, and sometimes it will fly to my window and tap at the glass!

More recently I have made contact with several people who seem to have the ability to communicate with animals on a deep soul level. Many believe that their animals 'talk' to them. It is fairly easy to work out when your dog wants to be taken for a walk or the cat wants to be fed, for example. In time we learn a whole range of symbols and signals which our pets give us to indicate their needs.

Some humans are becoming aware of their natural ability to connect with and to communicate with pets psychically. Holly is one of these. Holly is an animal communicator. Not only is she able to pick up information from animals in the usual way, she is also able to see picture messages from them, which goes much deeper than the way that most of us communicate with our pets. Holly can receive messages from dogs, cats and even horses who tell her information about themselves and their own well being, and also personal information about the owners themselves.

She works closely with the animals' own vet to help provide cures for ill health, often at the pets' own suggestion, and of course the owners themselves are stunned when their pets give Holly 'readings'. Holly's work has been well publicized in newspapers and magazines.

Holly's Story

My name is Holly and I live in south-west Wales. I started to work as a professional animal communicator around four years ago.

I've had many interesting adventures and conversations with my animal and bird friends and helpers. In 2004 I was approached by some animals who asked me if I was ready to be a voice for them. After all the amazing help and support they had given over the years how could I refuse!

Over this time I have had the honour of speaking with hundreds if not thousands of wonderful animals and they never cease to amaze me.

The warm, compassionate, forgiving natures they have literally bowl me over. Only last week I was speaking with a beautiful mare that had been imported from the continent. She told me how she had had an electric cattle prod used on her whilst she was there. I asked her how she felt about this and the people that had done this to her. She told me that she didn't hate them. She pitied and felt sorry for them because their hearts must be closed for them to be able to do such a thing without a thought or feeling.

In 2002 my conversations with animals began to change. They were still the same in many ways but a deeper knowing and understanding appeared to be coming from them. They started to speak of their owners, of other animals and of the world in general and of the mess we have all been getting ourselves into on this planet.

These furred and feathered messengers pass many communications to those who are listening, not only to help in our day-to-day lives, but also to speak of the future and of times when they hope that people will come to understand and respect them for the wonderful beings that they are.

Many of us find ourselves setting out looking for a certain type of animal and yet find ourselves drawn to others. When we go with our gut intuition the very animals who need to come to us find their way, often by very strange synchronicities playing out along the way.

Each of these wonderful beings comes with its own message and with its own teachings. In 1999 a wonderful mare by the name of Kayleigh came to me. She was very ill with a tumour which was operated on straight away. Over the coming years other health problems crept in and came to light. In 2004 things were much worse and she told me one day that her time had come but that she wanted to go into the field with her friends for a few days first.

For a long time I had been asking her how I could help her, that I needed her to stay with me and how I wanted to make her well.

Her answer was always the same ... 'Only you can make me better, you know how to make me well.'

For a long time I gave her everything she asked for yet she got worse and worse. Then the penny dropped, the way to make her well was to admit defeat and let her go ... to stop being selfish and stop trying to keep her with me and to give her what she needed most, which was her physical freedom.

As odd as it sounds, this was one of the most wonderful days of my life; that beautiful mare with her long flowing mane spoke to me so sincerely and with such compassion. We said everything that needed to be said and understood each other that day completely. In the days to follow she sent many messages to me through other people and animals. The e-mails, telephone calls and messages from animals passed via their human owners just didn't stop. They were all surrounding and supporting me every step of the way.

I had felt like my heart would break but the mare showed me who she really was. The essence of her; that all knowing, beautiful horse she was, not the ill body that stood before me. The day we said goodbye to her I was smiling, I was so happy for her, setting her free of her pain. Yet I still see her in the field with the others galloping around, she still speaks to me and guides me and holds my hand when I need that reassurance.

These winged messengers, these angels saved me? Yes, most certainly … every step of the way … without their wonderful help and understanding I would not be the person I am today, I may well have even gone down an entirely different route all together but these wonderful angels got me on track, helped me, taught me and set me on my right path.

Elizabeth is also an animal communicator who works very closely with animal energy.

Rubin

Not only can animals save your life but they can also save your sanity, give you strength and also courage. They help you to carry on when life brings you challenges; they lift the fog from your eyes, restoring your faith by showing unconditional, uncomplicated love with an inner sense of knowing …

I write from a place of first-hand experience because I own the most wonderful dog, named Rubin. Things had been difficult in my life for some time. I was a single parent living in a council flat with my one-year-old daughter Rachael. Then I met a man who promised me the world and within a year of meeting we married and moved into a nice terraced house.

Sadly, within a few days things began to go disastrously wrong and I realized I had made a huge mistake. I had married a person whom I began to fear.

I longed for something to love and someone to love me in return. I had always had pets but my husband refused my plea to get a dog. One evening while he was out working late, I went into the garden to fetch in some washing when I heard a meowing sound coming from our garden shed. I discovered a beautiful black cat stuck in there. The cat was very thin and very hungry, so I fed him and gave him a drink and left him outside hoping he would return home.

The cat ended up meowing outside the back door all night, until I eventually let him in. He was gentle and kind. We kept him for just over a week but due to my husband's disapproval, and me having a cat allergy, I was forced to rehome him.

The children were devastated. They had fallen in love with the cat but it did give me the courage to decide that I would go and get a dog that very day. The children and I needed a pet in our lives.

I drove to a local dog's home and explained that I needed a dog that would be very good with young children. They told me there was only one candidate, a small four-year-old brown Jack Russell–corgi cross. They let him out of his cold bare cage and he ran straight over and jumped up at my legs. In an instant I heard myself saying, 'I will take him.' I tried not to think of the consequences of taking him home.

My husband was not impressed and described my boy as plain and ordinary. I did not care, I had got him home, he was mine and I was not going to part with him for anybody. I renamed him Rubin and he settled in instantly. He loved the children and they loved him.

In the weeks that followed, my marriage became worse than ever but Rubin always defended me and licked away my tears.

One night things came to a head when my husband physically attacked me in our kitchen, placing his hands around my neck until I couldn't breathe. Rubin went ballistic and eventually my husband let go. If Rubin had not been there, I dread to think what might have happened …

Rubin gave me the strength to tell my husband to leave and he did that same night. I was not only devastated, but I also felt such a failure, with a heap of debt that my husband had hidden from me throughout our marriage.

The first few nights I felt broken and cried myself to sleep. I was unable to see a solution to our problems but knew that I had to carry on for the sake of the children. Rubin would hear my crying and jump on to the bed. He would actually climb in under the duvet and lie next to me with his head on the pillow beside mine. He then would put his paws around me and give me a cuddle!

We would stay like that most of the night and he comforted me and took away my pain. I feared that we would lose our home and I struggled to find enough money to feed the children, but thankfully due to a supportive family and our beloved Rubin, we got through it. He helped me mentally fight to keep the house, he gave me the strength to comfort and protect the children and he was there for all of us as a friend. I can honestly say that had he not been there, I would have not come through it the way I have.

I have been through many problems since this. Like many people I have had my fair share of problems like losing loved ones, illness and so on, but Rubin is always there for me, and instinctively knows when something is wrong.

My proudest day with Rubin was two years ago. My daughter and I took him to a local dog show and in a large class of approximately twelve other dogs, Rubin won the 'best veteran class'. How I cried when the judge handed my daughter the 'Winners' rosette. I was so proud of him, he has always been my winner.

Now he is fourteen years old, he is always at my side, he is my rock, my best friend, my saviour and my angel in disguise, and I dread the day when he physically leaves me. But I know in my heart that we will always be together, the bond is too strong to break.

Thank you Rubin for all you have done for me and my children. We are thankful that you are still with us

now to celebrate the good times that we are now
blessed to have.

Elizabeth is one of many people who feel connected
with their pets. Their love is unconditional. They are
living guardians and protectors who calm us by their
very presence. Can they talk to us? Yes, although not always in the way that we might expect. Elizabeth and
Holly receive messages directly from animals to pass on
to their owners but most of us are aware of simple communication from our own pets. They say that the dog is
(wo)man's best friend. Our animal friends are travelling
by our side in this life and the next, supporting us. They
never judge us and never question our choices and
ideas. They just love us. Now that sounds like an angel
to me!

CHAPTER 8

Loving Angels on This Side

The golden moments in the stream of life rush past
us and we see nothing but sand; the angels come to
visit us, and we only know them when they are gone.

George Eliot

A stranger who appears out of nowhere to help you change your car tyre; a stranger who warns you from driving home a particular way. Often these 'people' help you and then disappear as if they were never there. We have already seen some of these stories in earlier chapters. Sometimes it is hard to tell if we are being helped by strangers from this side or the other side.

Many times we might call a person 'an angel' and what we mean is that they are a kindly person who has gone above and beyond the call of duty to assist us or others. That person has helped us in a way that was almost unexpected in its generosity. In this case we feel that they are being guided and helped by the angels in their task.

When human beings are put under stressful situations they almost always come through. That is, they manage to stretch themselves in ways that even they themselves can hardly believe. Here is a collection of stories about loving angels on this side ... or are they? Bernadine D'-Sousa from Woodbridge, Virginia, wrote to share her magical Christmas story.

Christmas Angel

It was two weeks before Christmas in 1995. Bernadine's four-year-old daughter Jaime had been sick since late October, suffering from a wretched cough and chest congestion. But on this day, Jaime was extremely weak from the constant coughing.

The doctor diagnosed bronchitis, but worried it might be pneumonia and prescribed an antibiotic. 'We pumped her full of cough and cold medicines,' Bernadine said, 'But nothing helped her condition. I was so worried.' The doctor then suggested she might have tuberculosis.

Bernadine hugged her young daughter close to her as the doctor ordered her to drive to the hospital for a chest x-ray. Her husband was at work, and she felt totally alone as she walked with Jaime to the car.

'I cried as I drove,' Bernadine said. 'I asked God to please tell my why Jaime wasn't getting any better. Not knowing what was wrong with her was the worst part.'

At the hospital, Bernadine was seated next to an

older man who struck up a conversation with her. 'My heart was heavy with worry, and I didn't feel much like talking. He asked me why I was at the hospital so I told him about Jaime's cough and chest congestion. I was now worried we could lose her.'

The man turned to her and said his child had similar symptoms years ago and it turned out to be an allergy to the burning firewood in their fireplace.

Bernadine could have cried tears of joy. 'Suddenly, I felt a peaceful calm come over me. I knew at that instant that Jaime was allergic to the fumes from the firewood we often burned in our home,' Bernadine said. 'I picked up my child and left the hospital without ever getting the chest x-ray!'

Bernadine told her husband and they immediately stopped burning firewood. Jaime was well soon after. Bernadine said, 'I knew we had our answer when Jaime visited a friend who had a fire burning in the fireplace. She came home coughing and congested. It was a Christmas I will never forget. I can't remember what we got for material presents. We had received a much more magical gift.

'I know God sent that kind man to play angel for me. We must trust in God and know he will never let us down.'

This stranger helped to create an awakening. Sometimes this information from strangers seems to be passed from the very angels themselves with the strangers acting as messengers for the celestial realms. This awakening comes as a deep knowing which grows from within ourselves. Bernadine was aware instantly that the stranger's message gave her the information that she needed.

Julie Windsor from America wrote to me about her best friend Jeni who was seriously injured in a car accident. Julie heard the voice of her friend cut through the clear night.

A Voice from the Coma

Jeni was in a coma for more than a month, kept alive on a life support system. Her doctors gave her no chance for recovery from brain stem injuries, a crushed skull on the right side, and broken vertebrae in her back.

Jeni's family had given up hope and were planning her funeral. 'I overheard her relatives talking and saying how they thought the real Jeni, meaning her spirit, had left the hospital room,' Julie said. 'But for some reason, I could not give up on her.'

That night, Julie was lying in bed, trying to get to sleep about midnight.

'I heard Jeni's voice, saying "Julie, I'm still here. Don't give up on me yet like everyone else."'

The next day, Julie hurried to the hospital and told Jeni's family about the voice. This gave them a bit more faith and they asked the doctor to do another brain activity test. The doctors were ready to pull the plug, but instead they lowered the dosage of drugs that were supposed to reduce brain swelling.

Later that day, they detected blood flow to the brain and reduced the drug amount again. A few days later, Julie was talking to Jeni. 'I suddenly noticed her brow twitch. I knew she was coming back to us.'

Over the next week, Jeni moved more and more. Slowly, she awakened from her coma. Within a few weeks, she was walking and starting to regain her memory.

'It's been two years since that horrible accident,' Julie said. 'And we have our Jeni back. She now walks with a slight limp, but we are eternally grateful to have her in our lives.'

Julie told Jeni about the voice she heard that night. Jeni said she came because her best friend was the only one who hadn't given up on her. Jeni said a guardian angel had helped her find a way to speak to Julie.

Jeni was so grateful: 'Julie and the angel saved my life!'

A beautiful story of angels and humans working hand in hand!

A person is disposed to an act of choice by an angel ...
sometimes he is instructed by angelic illumination, both that
this act is good and as to the reason why it is good.

Saint Thomas Aquinas

Janet from America wrote to share her own experiences. Her stories show how we can all take it in turns to 'be an angel'.

Angels Watching over Me

There are angels among us ... earth angels. In a way we are all angels to the people we come in contact with every day. I know many people refer to me as 'an angel' which is a wonderful feeling. But I know there have been many angels surrounding me in the past five to six months.

I became very depressed and wanted to end it all after I lost a long-time job and had to move back with my parents at nearly twenty-eight years old. My mother constantly criticized my choices, and made me feel lower than the dirt I walked on.

I remember one day that I was driving around after a bad argument the night before with my mom and I basically hit rock bottom. I was waiting at a railroad crossing for the train to go by and was thinking that getting hit by the train might be the way out that I was looking for. But a song came on the radio ... 'Let me be the one you call, when you jump I'll break your fall … if you need to crash then crash and burn, you're not alone.'

I started to cry and realized that I wasn't alone at all. I realized later on that an angel made sure I didn't go through with my plans because he knew that I was going to make it after all.

I know there have been angels around me many times because I have hit rock bottom more than once. When I shared my feelings with others, those people were so supportive and told me, 'Everything will be okay … you are a great person, you are wonderful, you are caring,' and so on. I wish I knew how the angels realize when I need to hear a particular song or songs at a certain time. I think an angel has a hand in it and told those radio people to 'Play those "Savage Garden" songs for Janet because she needs to hear the messages and be soothed.'

I was told I was 'an angel' by a young woman I helped myself a few months ago. She was in a similar situation to mine and was suffering from depression. I kept emailing her and even posted on the web-boards begging people to help me help her.

She decided not to end it all, and was so grateful for my help. When the tables were turned, and I needed a friend, she was one of the first people to come to my aid too. Angels on earth can be of any age. They can be male or female. They are from different countries, different backgrounds, and so on. In a way we are angels on earth to those we come into contact with, either on the internet or in person. Someday I want to meet those people who are my angels on earth and thank them for being there, being supportive, and telling me I am going make it through life's obstacles.

The internet has opened up the whole world. I have several 'angel friends' of my own from countries all over the world. Many of these people I have never met but they have provided me with the support that I have needed over the years when family and friends were unable to help. Our internet friends can be available at inconvenient times of night due to the time difference across the world. There is always someone 'online' who is able and willing to listen to you. What a fantastic invention. I have a dear friend who is unable to leave her home at all. The internet is her life and without it she would have no human contact for much of the day.

When you work from home as I do, these internet friends take on even greater meaning. They become your very 'work colleagues' and there are friends to suit every diverse interest one might have. If you find difficulty making friends then consider making an internet friend and join a regular online group or club; it's a great way to increase confidence and get you started.

Here is another story of strangers appearing from nowhere. Kelly was assisted by a stranger whom she believes saved her from scarring. In typical angel style the 'angel' disappeared soon after the incident and was not seen ever again.

Saved from Scarring

When I was about twenty-one I had a very old Ford Fiesta with a faulty radiator. Whilst I was in traffic, it seemed to overheat so I pulled over into a car park and stupidly tried to fix it.

I took the cap off and basically the boiling hot water came gushing out and right into my face. A man came from nowhere and chucked cold water over me, which I was later told saved my face from scarring. He then walked me to the hospital.

As soon as I walked in they whisked me into a cubical and attended to me straight away. All I remember is the man saying, 'Everything will be all right now,' then disappearing.

After a while I asked the nurse to get him to thank him but he had gone. I never managed to get his name or ask where he came from and he did not seem to have an accent or any way of my identifying him.

Mum and I think he may have been one of my guardian angels!

Sounds familiar, doesn't it? Joyce is from Scotland. She wrote to me following my request for angel stories.

Crossing the Road

During the mid-nineties, before I realized I was a psychic medium and healer, I was saved by angels. I have no doubt whatsoever.

When I was just eight years old, I was knocked down in a serious road accident. I always take great care crossing the road nowadays, many times preferring to wait until there are no cars on the go at all before I will cross.

One clear afternoon I had done just this, but as I was about to cross the busy road in my home town of Edinburgh I did my usual check both ways. I had a clear view of the traffic both coming and going. Deciding the road was clear, I lifted my foot to step off the kerb when to my surprise, a man (a total stranger to me) appeared from nowhere at my side, and without a word, placed his hand flat across my stomach!

I was so surprised at his action, I literally stopped my foot, leaving it hanging in mid air, to look firstly at his hand, and then at him. The man was very short, bald and plump, and dressed very simply. As I looked at the man, a car also seemed to appear from nowhere. It was moving at great speed. The car passed in front of me, right in the spot where my foot would have been if I had lifted it down into the road as I had intended. As I turned to thank the man, he had disappeared.

It makes you want to say, 'Oh yes, another story like that.' Yet these stories happen often years apart to people from different countries and they come from people who have nothing in common and have never even met! It makes you realize that there is a serious pattern emerging here.

Heidy's angel certainly played his role to perfection when she asked him to help her on a special search. Remember the 'praying' stories earlier? This story also includes that magical element.

Missing

Back in March, 2002, my partner Tony gave me a beautiful £900 engagement ring. I was so excited! I wanted to show my friends up at the local school but the ring was just a little too big – that wasn't going to stop me so I decided to wear it anyway! I had a lot of fun and kept waving my fingers around and pretending to yawn so that they would notice my gorgeous ring.

Later that evening, at around 6 pm, I looked at my hand and was stunned to discover that my ring was missing. I was horrified. I just ran around the house checking everywhere, even in the bins. I even unscrewed the u-bend in the kitchen sink and stuck my fingers in the soggy stuff that had caught at the bottom but it wasn't there.

I just didn't know what to do but I was sure that this wasn't a celestial sign. There was nothing else for it but to just pray so I went up to my room and knelt down.

'Oh God, please help me to find my ring ... if Tony is the man for me, then please help me.'

I walked halfway down the stairs and became really calm. I felt as if someone was with me, guiding me in some way, so I put on my shoes and coat. Tony was calm and told me not to worry. He just felt it had been lost for good but I was determined and said to him, 'I'm not coming back until I find it.'

Three other schools had come out after the time that my own children's school had finished but I just felt that I might still find it somehow. Tony had prepared the children for my return and told them that I would be really upset and that they must be especially good when I got back ...

I walked slowly, checking everywhere along the route. I called in at a couple of shops that I had visited earlier but no one had seen my beautiful new ring. I was so close to tears.

I walked right up to the school and became aware of a man on the other side of the road. He was just standing there so I assumed he was waiting for a lift. I walked all the way up to the school gates and my ring was nowhere to be seen, but I was still sure it would turn up. As I began my walk home I still kept my eyes on the ground and as I got to the corner, there was my ring ... right in the middle of the path. As I picked it up I almost exploded with joy and at the same time, noticed that the man was still standing on the opposite pavement.

I lifted my head up to the sky to say thank you out loud and even blew a kiss which made me feel a little silly! I looked round to see if the man had seen me but he had vanished. I feel sure that the strange man must have had something to do with my ring appearing at that moment … it sure wasn't just a 'coincidence' and I know I had searched every area of that path. At any rate, I had my answer and Tony and I married five months later.

Sometimes our angel is human but their assistance makes them momentarily something above and beyond a 'mere human'. A gesture can be small or large but that flash in time makes more than an earthly difference to our life.

The last story in this chapter is very different to the others. William Wayne Sinclair will never forget his human angel. At one of the most tragic incidents of recent times, many humans performed great and wondrous acts of bravery. Each of these people has said they were only 'doing their duty' or 'doing what any other human would have done in the same situation'. Not every human being, to be sure! This story is a tribute to them all.

My 9/11 Guardian Angel

On 11 September 2004 I was sitting at my desk on the first floor D Ring of the Pentagon, when flight 77 crashed into the building at 9:37:46. I remember very clearly the loud explosion caused by the jet fuel-fed fire. Thick black smoke filled the air ...

The walls, ceiling, desk and computers were thrown up into the air, and many people working in the office were thrown to the floor. It was terrifying. I was completely covered with jet fuel, fire and debris and the smoke was so thick and black that it was impossible to see which way to go.

The walls had been completely blown out and since the walls were gone there was no way to get a bearing on which way was the way out. I had no idea what to do. Suddenly, through the smoke, fire, and the calling for help, I heard a voice calling louder than the rest, 'If you can hear me, head towards my voice.' Was this even a real person?

I didn't hang around to find out but began to follow the sound of the voice. Other colleagues too tracked the voice of hope, calling out of the darkness and leading us out of the burning building. When we got outside we were stunned at the devastation all around us. In the confusion I searched for the person behind the voice but search as I might, I could not see, or hear anyone calling.

A few weeks after I was released from the hospital, a lady called me at home. She said that she had read an article about me in the *Washington Post*. She was particularly interested to hear about the voice and the phrase I had heard on that tragic day. You can imagine how stunned I was when she said, 'I think it was my husband that was calling out.'

Later that same day I received a phone call from a Pentagon police officer, who told me he was the one who called out to us. At last I had found my guardian angel and I told him that he had certainly saved my life that day.

A week or so later we eventually met and I was thrilled to meet him at the Channel 4 studio in Washington, DC, and since that day we have met several more times. I even invited him and his family to our family reunion. We have become the best of friends since then and I truly believe that he is my Guardian Angel.

Ordinary folk become 'honorary guardian angels' by performing extraordinary acts of bravery and courage to assist others in need. Take this message out into the world and be an angel yourself whenever the opportunity arises.

CHAPTER 9

Children's Angels

Matthew, Mark, Luke and John,
The bed be blest that I lie on.
Four angels to my bed,
Four angels round my head,
One to watch, and one to pray,
And two to bear my soul away.

Thomas Ady, A Candle in the Dark

... The Angels were all singing out of tune, and hoarse
with having little else to do, excepting to wind up the sun
and moon or curb a runaway young star or two.

Lord Byron

If we do nothing else we must teach children to 'ask'
their angels for help and protection. Many children are
comforted by knowing that their angels watch over
them at night. Asking their angels for help and thanking
them for their care can be as much a bedtime ritual as
prayers and bedtime stories. I always did this with my

own children and they never suffered the nightmares that other children of their age did (including me). I know it helped them.

Children who are told about angels are more confident in working with their own guardians. Many children see angels regardless of whether others around them believe that they do, but imagine how much easier it is to talk about their own encounters and beliefs if parents and grandparents are open and receptive? Children can be very psychic indeed.

Angels can be very powerful visions which carry us through our deepest darkest hours. James went through the most terrible abuse as a child but was comforted by his guardian angel although he wasn't sure at the time what had happened. James was kind enough to write and share his personal story.

Safe

I am a fifty-year-old man now but as a child I was abused by my father and remember this clearly still. One day when I was just three year old I was being comforted by my mother after a severe beating. The strange thing about this experience though is that every time I think about it I realize that I am always watching myself being comforted and could never understand why. I know that I am watching this happen from the other side of the room.

A few weeks ago I saw your book *An Angel Treasury* and bought it because I have a great interest in angels. I had only glanced at it when it 'fell' off the shelf and landed on my toes. I got the message and decided to read the book properly! When I read the part about angels taking the spirit of abused children from their bodies, the tears flowed from me. I now know why I see myself from the other side of the room. Thank you.

It's true. I have heard from many who were lifted from their spiritual bodies temporarily whilst they were in physical danger. Sharing these stories does help to comfort others almost as if they've had the angel encounter themselves.

Nicola had a couple of experiences when she was a child. In the first one her Nana was her 'angel'. It's sad when parents don't believe their children's experiences but many people are more open to these things nowadays. Information is available on the internet and more books are covering such experiences, so we do have a better understanding.

Nana Visits

My nana passed on in the early 1980s during the Easter break. I was really upset and even though I knew she was really ill, her passing still hit me hard. It's taken me a long time (a very long time) to get over it but I know she's okay now.

Several years later, my little sister was ill in bed with measles. I had all the symptoms, except for the spots, and I was having trouble sleeping. I was crying as all kids do when they're ill. I'd managed to settle down for a sleep when I was woken by the feeling of someone sat on my feet. When I looked, there was my nana! Part of me was really happy because she was there but then I got frightened because I knew she 'couldn't be there' because she was dead, so I pulled the covers over my head.

She was just sitting on the end of my bed, smiling at me, as solid as if she was really there. I remember peeking out and telling her that I loved her dearly but she'd have to go now because she was scaring me. She just smiled all the more, nodded once and was gone again – just as if she'd stood up.

I told my mum the next morning and she said it was just because I was poorly, but I'm not convinced it was. I know my nana was sat on my bed that night. Then later I had another similar experience …

On the night that my cousin Paul died, I was having a nice dream (totally un-family linked) when Paul popped in and said, 'Goodbye'. I woke up with a start and realized a commotion was going on in my parents' living room. There was a woman there wailing about something but she was so upset I couldn't hear what was being said.

My mum came upstairs to check on my sister and me. My sister was asleep and I wasn't. I asked what was going on and my mum told me that something had happened to Paul and that she and my dad (and the wailing woman) would be heading off round the corner to my Aunt's house. I asked what had happened to Paul and Mum replied, 'There's been an accident,' but we weren't to say anything to my sister.

I knew then why he'd said goodbye. As my parents and the woman (who was his fiancée's mother) left, I heard talking from my sister's room. I went in and she was sat up in bed, and as the door opened she turned to look at it and saw me. Looking back to her right, she shrugged, then asked me if I'd seen where Paul had gone because he'd woken her up to talk. We both told Mum in the morning and she said we were making it up.

Of course this is a typical reaction to children's angel experiences although nowadays, with more information available, more parents are tolerant of their children's paranormal experiences.

There is still little information about for parents. One fantastic book is *The Psychic Power of Children*, by Cassandra Eason. Cassandra has included one of my own childhood paranormal experiences in her book and I know that she has a lot of experience in this area. Cassandra's own children have had many psychic experiences between them and she shared this angel story with me.

Angel at the Window

My son Jack was about six years old when one day he looked out of the bedroom window and said, quite matter-of-factly, 'Mum there's an angel outside the window.'

Naturally, I couldn't see anything so I asked him to describe the angel. 'What does the angel look like?' I asked him casually.

'You know,' he said impatiently, 'it's got wings and a halo, like an angel!'

Then because he had reached the age when he was questioning everything he asked me if I thought it was a clockwork angel because it was flying.

Trying to be helpful I suggested that maybe it was a fairy. He looked at me as if I was being really stupid and said patiently, 'Angels are angels and fairies are fairies!'

Then he rapidly lost interest. 'Can I have some crisps?' he said, as if nothing had happened.

To Jack angels were a fact of life, and he said he had seen them before. The only reason he mentioned it now was because he was curious about how they might be propelled.

I spoke to Cassandra about her feelings over the lack of support that children have and she told me:

I get letters from people in their eighties who tell me that they were never believed or sometimes punished for telling of a psychic experience they had in childhood. Hopefully over the sixteen or so years I have been researching the subject there is more openness, but sadly not always among health professionals and psychologists. What worries me is that we talk to quite young children about drugs, sex and alcohol, yet psychic experience, though common and normal, is still taboo.

I agree with Cassandra, and have tried to open up access to information myself. For some while now I have been running an online support group for parents of psychic children so that parents can swap ideas and coping strategies. I believe some of the best help can come from other parents in the same situation.

You can access this support group by visiting my website (www.jackynewcomb.co.uk). With so many children being born with the ability to see angels and the previously 'unseen world' we will become more accustomed to the phenomenon as our understanding grows.

This next story is totally shocking. Can you imagine the horror of hearing that your schoolgirl daughter has been pronounced dead? That is what happened to Jackie Lynch from County Galway.

Pronounced Dead

On the morning of 6 November 2002, my daughter Georgia, who was just twelve years old, set off for school as normal. She didn't have a care in the world.

But at 12.30 that afternoon, I had the worst telephone call in my whole life. Georgia's school rang to tell me that she had stopped breathing! I can't begin to tell you the panic I felt inside, and just dropped everything and ran in the direction of the school.

When I reached the school, Georgia had been pronounced dead. I just couldn't believe it. How could my lovely daughter be dead? Her life had just begun.

As I looked around I could see the total chaos around me. Georgia was being given mouth-to-mouth resuscitation by a fourteen-year-old girl. There were priests in the room, two nuns, and two ambulances had now arrived. Lots of people seemed to be just standing around watching. Everything seemed too unreal but eventually Georgia was put in the ambulance and the medics took over. She was totally blue and lifeless on the way to the hospital. What had happened? The crew told me that my little girl had had a brain haemorrhage and there was very little hope.

When we arrived at the hospital it was like something from the television programme *ER*. Everyone was running around like crazy and just jumped into action. My husband Geoff, Georgia's dad, had also arrived by now.

We were both stood there in shock. Georgia was put onto life support but then it was decided that she should be flown by helicopter to Beaumont hospital in Dublin.

They couldn't really tell us anything but we were told on numerous occasions that it was only the machines that were keeping her alive. The pain we felt inside was unimaginable, and raw. I just felt like I was working on autopilot.

Eventually, after two days and two nights of sitting by her bed, we had to rest, so we agreed to go back to Geoff's sister, have a bath and get some sleep while my dad and sister-in-law continued the vigil by her bed. I felt better for the bath, change of clothes and hot chocolate. We were no sooner in bed when Geoff fell immediately into a deep sleep. I was just lying there tossing and turning although I was so tired. I knew we could be contacted if we were needed because our two mobile phones were beside the bed.

All of a sudden, with no warning, a bright light came straight through the window, and there at the end of our bed was the most beautiful angel. I couldn't believe my eyes. The name Petra came to me, and I was told in my mind that she was a guardian angel! As I looked up to her face, she gave me the most amazing smile and at that moment I felt so at peace. Slowly the light faded from the room. I turned to look at the phones, and I honestly expected them to ring with news of Georgia's passing, but the phones didn't ring and shortly afterwards I too drifted off to sleep.

By the morning, the anticipated bad news still hadn't come, and although Georgia stayed in a coma for three weeks, and had many ups and downs along the way, she did eventually make a full recovery. Georgia was back at school six months later, and now at fifteen, is almost like any other teenager her age. There's not a day goes by when I don't thank Petra, and light a candle for her and Georgia.

Nobody thought I was crazy when I told them about my angel visit, and we were very grateful that there was such a happy ending.

Georgia said her only memory or dream, of those few weeks that she was unconscious was living under the sea, and swimming with fishes! Some people during near death experiences (experiencing clinical death and the spiritual body leaving the physical body) go through 'healing waters' or 'showers of light' during their heavenly visits, so there may be more to this than meets the eye! We also see again here the bright white light phenomenon!

Part 3

CHAPTER 10

Love from the Other Side

Yes, love indeed is light from heaven; a spark of that
immortal fire with angels shared, by Allah given to
lift from earth our low desire.

Lord Byron

Are our loved ones angels? Well, not in the strictest
sense of the definition, but they certainly act as our angels. Our loved ones often retain their earthly
personalities when they cross into the light. They are
our loved ones as we remember them – but they now
have a wider spiritual understanding of our world.

Some people believe that our loved ones have the ability to see slightly into our future, they have access to the
spiritual libraries or Akashic Records (or the book of life)
as it is sometimes called. Many of the comforting and life-
saving visitation messages seem to bear this theory out.
They come back to warn us of danger in our future.

Do remember, though, that these messages from our
loved ones are like visiting a psychic for a reading. Our

'future' is only a likely future outcome based on our current set of circumstances. So, if you are warned to drive carefully in a red car and you don't even go out that day, then you are not going to be any more at risk than on other days. How much you take notice of these messages is a personal choice (we have our own free will) but it's always nice to have a 'little help from our friends!'

Of course, these spirit relatives don't suddenly have the answers to everything. If Aunt Edith didn't approve of your boyfriend when she was on this side of life but you knew her judgement was flawed, she might still feel the same on the other side and it doesn't suddenly make her the fountain of all knowledge!

On the other hand, relatives who cared deeply for us when they were with us on earth are still going to care deeply for us when they cross over. Love is eternal. They also have a deeper insight into our feelings and are aware of when we are sad and grieving. Often they come back just to comfort us even though they are aware that there is no such thing as 'time' in the spiritual realms where they currently exist (not in the way that we understand it anyway). They know that we will all be together again soon but do 'get' that we cannot understand that.

We miss our loved ones deeply but their greatest wish is that we continue to live and thrive after their passing. They 'come back' in visions and dreams to reassure us that they are okay. Not all spirits have the ability to do this and for most of them the knack of manifesting in our reality, even for a brief moment, is a difficult task (rather like us trying to take ourselves out of our own body to appear briefly in their realms).

This is why as human beings so many people report seeing their loved ones during a near-death experience or when their body has been traumatized in some way (following an operation or an accident, for example), because we are momentarily in a different state of awareness (like when we are asleep, meditating or unconscious).

In the days and weeks following physical death, many people report visits (a spirit visitation) from their loved ones. In this period when the spirit is still close to the earthly realms it is easier for them to make this communication.

Children will often be the ones to receive the messages and words of comfort (especially young children), because naturally our own physical grief can block these messages from coming through. Here is an example of the messages that reach us, miracles in every sense of the word. Kathy shares her story.

Goodnight Love

My mother came to me the night after she died. It was something I will never forget ...

My mother became ill on a Saturday night. I'm from Northern Ireland but I was living in Guernsey at the time which made things more traumatic. I didn't hear about my mother's illness until the Sunday and by this time she was already seriously ill and in hospital. The family were great and called me regularly throughout the day to keep me up to date, but I could see that the situation was bad.

Naturally I was desperate to get a flight home to Belfast to be with everyone but I couldn't get one until the following morning. In the end I telephoned the hospital myself and spoke to the sister who said that she had been expecting my call. It was very sad and the sister gently explained that my mother wasn't expected to live through the night. She only had an hour or two left to live so I knew I wouldn't get to say goodbye, which was very distressing for me.

I explained the situation to the sister about the flights and she warned me to stay by the phone. I stayed home all day and night and by the next morning I still hadn't had a telephone call from the family. Eventually my sister called me and the family were all surprised that my mother had hung on for so long. My aunt felt that mum was waiting for me. Mum was not really aware of people around her now so it was clear that she was slipping away.

Finally, my flight arrived and I went straight to the hospital. The family were all in a different room so I was able to go in and see mum on my own. When I got to her bedside she appeared to be sleeping. I sneaked a look at her monitor but when I looked down at her again she was watching me.

'What are you doing home?' she asked me, so I told her I had just slipped in for a visit.

She was very lucid up to that point and just asked me to tell the rest of the family to let her sleep as she was so tired. As I walked out of the room she was smiling and waving to me so I smiled and waved back. Just fifteen minutes later she died.

Later on that night I went back to our family home alone, and I climbed into my mother's bed. I distinctly heard her voice call out to me, 'Goodnight love,' and it was almost like an echo.

Then a few years later she appeared in a dream. I was at a wedding and was taking photographs when I noticed an extra person standing on the edge of the group. It was my mum. It was an unusual dream because I was aware that I was dreaming, and knew that I was the only person who could see her.

She took me by the hand and I went flying with her. We flew over houses in our neighbourhood and I remember thinking in my dream that if anyone could see me they would think I was barmy and talking to myself. Like before, I was aware that this was a dream but also that it was real.

All too soon it was time for her to leave, and as she drifted off I asked her a question. She did shout the answer back to me, but sadly by this time she was too far away for me to hear her. I know that this was real.

These spirit visitations, where our loved ones appear in dreams, are classified by this phenomenon of us 'knowing' we are in a dream (lucid dreaming) but being aware of our loved ones, and the whole experience being 'very real'. We are conscious, but on another level (more like a deep meditative state). Another thing that happens is that these dream type experiences never fade and people remember all the details even years later. And of course, the 'flying' is the out-of-body experiences which I learnt myself. Oh how I wish my own loved ones would come and take me flying too!

Here is Rachel's experience.

Safe with My Dog

My father died two years ago this July. Just after he died I kept waking up because I could feel someone in my room. It was my dad and he told me not to worry because he was with his dog Bess and his parents on the other side.

Sara and her family had a visit from a very special person on New Year's Day. Sara's dad William was known to the family as Ted. He was just sixty-three when he died last February. Ted had been ill with angina; he'd had heart bypasses and was diabetic, although naturally it was still a shock when he passed.

Happy New Year

My dad had been living at our old home in Bristol. Mum and Dad had separated, and I lived with my mum in Lympsham. Mum and I had a phone call late one night to say that Dad had had a heart attack and it was bad. They asked us to go to the hospital in Bristol. We made it in enough time to see him and say our goodbyes. Only the machines were keeping him alive, and we had to make the horrible decision to turn them off. After Dad passed I kept getting upset that I couldn't see him.

Christmas was the worst time because Dad used to make a real big deal of Christmas celebrations. He was a chef and he'd cook wonderful meals.

For a long while I kept a box with things related to Dad until recently I felt able to part with the box. I still keep a couple of photos of him in my bedroom.

I remember one occasion when I was in hospital having my appendix out I was by myself waiting to be operated on and I saw the indentation on the chair next to me. I was sure that it was Dad because he had always been with me when I was in hospital before. I have a photo of me and Mum on my twenty-first birthday with a vortex-like thing over Mum's shoulder. It is as if Dad had jumped into the photograph with us.

The most memorable time was New Year.

Mum, myself and Rob my boyfriend were sitting watching television and bringing in the New Year. It was around twelve thirty in the morning when we heard a noise in the house. It sounded like something heavy had hit the floor. I went to investigate and discovered that one of my dad's ornaments had fallen over. Nothing had dropped on it and I could see no explanation as to why it had happened. It was the first ornament on the shelf so nothing could have knocked it. It made us all a bit goosepimply, even Rob.

I like to think it was Dad's way of saying Happy New Year from the other side. I had been talking about how much I love and miss him just the day before so maybe that was something to do with it.

Mum said straight away that it was Dad's way of saying Happy New Year. The next day when Rob was on his way back home she said she thought that he was telling us he also approved of Rob.

As I am writing this it brings to mind something that happened to me last night. I was thoroughly absorbed in reading a fairy book that Rob had bought me for Christmas, when my CD system came on all on its own. I always turn it off at night, but when it switched on it made quite a noise before immediately turning itself back off again. I'm not really sure why it happened but I do feel like there was someone else in the room. It was a nice feeling and I went to sleep not long after it happened. These experiences have made me realize that this is Dad's way of getting through.

Sometimes our visitors can cause a little confusion, especially if their visit is unexpected or our visitor arrives in a way we are not expecting, like Andrew's dad.

Andrew's dad appeared looking at the peak of health, and this is a classic phenomenon of spirit visitations. I had a family friend visit me in a dream and although she was of retirement age when she passed, with greying hair, she looked like a younger woman with a shock of jet black hair! When I looked at photographs of her in her younger years I realized that this was exactly how she had looked once.

Here is Andrew's story.

A Younger Dad

About two or three weeks after my beloved father passed away in 2000 I had an experience where I was 'awoken from my sleep'. I was not an adult when I woke up but strangely I was only about eight years of age. (I'm actually thirty-eight).

I was back in the old box room of our family home where I shared a double bed with my twin sister. She was asleep beside me. The decor and blankets were the same as I remembered them. I saw a young man standing at the foot of the bed. He appeared to be in his late twenties or early thirties and he was dressed in a black suit with a crisp white shirt and black tie. The colours appeared very sharp. He was just standing there smiling at me.

I kept looking at the man and knew that I knew him. The person at the end of the bed was solid, and three dimensional. Something in my mind told me that this was my father but for some reason I didn't recognize him as the father I knew in 2000, and who was an old man at the age of seventy when he died.

I tried to call and nudge my sister but she was in a deep sleep and couldn't hear me. I could feel her body as I tried to nudge her to wake her up. I kept saying, 'Why has Dad sent his brother to me? Why has his brother come to me?'

The figure smiled even more as if he knew something that I didn't and was amused by my confusion and innocence. I noticed that he had beautiful teeth which were a feature of my father in his young days. He had a fine crop of jet black hair combed back in a1960s style. He also had very penetrating eyes. I could actually feel my heart pounding whilst all of this was going on, although there was a peace about this person. I eventually fell back to sleep.

It wasn't until the next day that I realized that the person standing at the end of the bed was indeed my father. He was dressed as he always dressed in his young days and was wearing a very nice suit. My mother was forever telling us how he had his suits made to measure and that although he worked as a welder in the Rover Works in Birmingham he was known by his workmates as 'the executive'. His teeth which were immaculate in the dream were another feature which my mother always used to comment on.

I was annoyed with myself for not taking full advantage of the experience and taking the opportunity to have a chat. But of course, I hadn't immediately realized it was my father. I don't really remember my father as he was in 1960s as I was only a toddler and have very few memories of that time. It's no wonder I didn't recognize him.

There must be some truth in the idea that when we die we take on the appearance of the best years of our lives. This would explain my 'dreams' where my parents always appear to be young. And may they stay forever young.

In this next story, Barbara's spiritual guardians gave her an announcement:

The Blue Flowers

Back in 1981 I was pregnant with my third child. I already had two sons whom I absolutely adored. My first birth was a caesarean. I am fairly small boned and he was a pretty big baby, lying in a breach position. The doctor felt this procedure would be safest for us both.

My second son was born two years later. He came early, and because he was distressed during labour I was advised to go for an emergency caesarean.

Although both of us survived, my son suffered a very stressful time in those early weeks of life. He had two collapsed lungs and I was told no baby had ever survived such an ordeal. He went down in the medical books at the time.

Naturally, having had two caesareans I was advised that it would be unwise to have more than three children (no question asked next time, the third birth would have to be another caesarean as the original scar could rupture).

With my third pregnancy I so desperately wanted a girl to complete my three-child family. I went and painted the nursery pink, and even went so far as to buy some pink girlie baby things … I so badly wanted a girl!

At around six months I went to sleep and had a beautiful dream-like experience. I was presented with a beautiful bunch of blue flowers. These flowers were exquisite, like nothing I had ever seen. The only way to describe them is by saying that each flower seemed to be lit up like a warm-glowing miniature light bulb – it is so hard to describe; they were out of this world. With the presentation of the flowers I had the calm feeling of knowing my baby was going to be a boy (although no words were spoken in the dream). I woke with a happy feeling, and just 'knew' it had been a message from the spirits.

I did go on to have my third son, and he is a joy and a credit to our family. I have no regrets at having another boy.

Against all the odds and the doctor's advice I did go on to have two more children. The last two pregnancies really brought my health down though, and if it wasn't for my mum and husband's help I don't think I would have carried either to full term.

I always had a feeling that I would have a girl. My fourth child was another boy, whom again I loved to bits. With this fourth pregnancy I was convinced it would be another boy (I did not have any more dreams to tell me either way). I decided to be sterilized after my fifth baby as I could not trust myself not to have another try if it was a boy again!

Lo and behold I got there in the end and finally had my girl.

All of my children are wonderful and we have always been a very close, loving family. I still recall being given those flowers at a time when I thought it was my last attempt at having a girl child. They remain very clear in my mind.

Gordon Gilmore firmly believes in angels and had amazing contact with his wife through a psychic medium after she passed.

An Angel's Time

Because the existence of angels has moved beyond a belief system into a reality for me, I would often tell my ailing wife that there are angels whose specific job it is to help the souls of humans cross over to the spirit realms.

Soon after my wife passed into Spirit, I searched for, and found, an experienced and genuine psychic medium so I could gather information on my wife's transition into Spirit. I was very fortunate to have my wife come through herself during my session with the medium, and these are the exact words she spoke of her transition into Spirit.

'As I rose from my body I saw an angel directly in front of me surrounded by a brilliant light. The angel was smiling and happy to see me and was beckoning for me to come. To the left of the angel were two ladies and a man weeping with joy. They were my mother, grandmother and father. Then I felt peaceful, warm and good as my mother hugged me. I then looked back at my body lying on the floor but the angel took me by the shoulder and said, "You are done there," and we walked into the Light. You spoke of angels to me, but I doubted their existence – now I know they are real.'

Kerry wrote to share her story with me after hearing me talk at an alternative health show. I often receive e-mails and letters from people following my talks and workshops and it's nice to see how people become aware of experiences in their own life and, in some cases, feel able to share their own stories which they had previously felt the need to suppress.

I have heard so many afterlife communication stories now that none of these stories scares or frightens me. Our relatives and friends from the other side continue to express love as they did in life.

Grandad's Visit

A friend of mine and I attended one of your talks recently at the Natural Living show in Birmingham which I thoroughly enjoyed. My friend was going through a really bad patch and I think your talk really helped her. Thank you.

I have always believed in an afterlife and angels and so on, as I have experienced many strange things since childhood and often receive information through dreams and thoughts for other people, which I pass on to them as often as I can.

Just over two years ago I believe I had some sort of confirmation. I would like to tell you because the people who I have told about this think I am barmy!

Just under three years ago my grandad was diagnosed with cancer and spent the remaining time of his life in hospital. Whilst in hospital Grandad kept telling my mom that her mother (his wife), who had died about thirty years previously, was visiting him at 6pm, 7pm and 8pm every night, saying that if he went with her he would be safe.

After about four weeks of being diagnosed, my mom called me to say he had been heavily sedated and that he probably wouldn't talk again, however the doctors had said that he had a strong heart and he would carry on for at least a few more weeks.

When I got to the hospital that night my mom asked me to talk to Grandad because 'I would know what to say.' I was really upset and didn't really know what my mom was expecting of me. I was also nervous as other family members were in the room as well so I went and sat with my grandad and just held his hand. I suddenly felt very calm and even though he was sedated, I felt he could hear me so for some reason I said to him, 'When she comes for you again, don't be scared, go with her.' When I said this, he made some sort of noise and gestured. I was positive he was trying to explain that he understood.

I asked my mom the time and it was about 7.15. I told them all he would go at 8.00. Smack bang on 8.00 my grandad died! Everybody was stunned; even me, and I have since been asked how I knew. I don't have any idea how or why I told Grandad and the other family members what I did, apart from the timing of my grandmother's visits to him.

Looking back it seems quite morbid to tell a room full of people an exact time at which someone is going to die. My mom, however, felt comforted by it. I have always felt that I know my grandmother, even though she died before I was born, as I am able to tell my mom things about her, so maybe she was telling me what to say.

I 'dreamt' about Grandad several times in the weeks after he passed and do believe that they were real visits. A few months later (in the winter), I was at home alone and felt very cold. I opened my bedroom curtains and the window was open very slightly. This seemed very strange as I never have the windows open in winter because I feel the cold, but I assumed my boyfriend had opened it. This still confused me because if he had opened the window, it would have been open for about three days (he didn't live with me and I hadn't seen him in that time).

After that I found the window open again and again, and each time I assumed it was my boyfriend. About a month later I opened the curtains one morning and the window was slightly open on the catch. This time I was a bit freaked. I live on my own and do check windows, doors, etc. before I go to bed, so this time I knew it was something else. I had started to smell cigarettes in my house which I didn't understand as I don't smoke (and people don't smoke in my house.)

Later I discussed this with my mom and she said straight away that it was my grandad. He had been blind when he was alive and lived on the ground floor of a warden-controlled block of apartments. Mom said that when he had a cigarette he used to open the window slightly and put it on the catch as he lived on the ground floor. That made a lot of sense and I no longer felt afraid. I instinctively knew it was Grandad, and thanked him for letting me know he was there. But I also asked him not to open the windows as it did freak me out a bit because I live on my own. Unbelievably, since telling my mom this she has experienced the same thing at her house.

I do believe my grandad is around me and often feel his presence. I feel closer to him now than when he was alive. On the anniversary of his death we had a bad fire at my mom's house. Something (or someone) woke her up and got her out of the house. We believe it was Grandad.

The announcement of the passing time is something I have experienced myself. My own grandmother had been ill for several weeks and I had sat with her for many hours each day. On her last day, I just knew it was the day of her passing and we had a special goodbye. When my sister later popped in for a visit I warned her that our grandmother would be passing over later on that day and I suggested she said goodbye.

'I've said goodbye,' she told me, looking confused.

'No, I don't mean say goodbye. I mean say GOOD-BYE.'

This time she understood me and went back into the room for a final visit. I guess this information comes from a higher soul level.

During the night my mother telephoned me to say that my grandmother had passed on as predicted and I ran around the corner to my mum and dad's house so that I could sit with my grandmother one last time.

The room felt calm and still and I kissed her goodbye. Her presence was in the room with us and we decided to drink a glass of sherry and toast her on her way. It sounds morbid but it was the most amazing experience you can imagine. I was so excited for her that she was passing over to the light – going home to be with the relatives she had talked about in the days before her passing. It was her time.

Hilary's grandfather, grandmother and father are regular visitors and the family are not afraid at all. With this story a little humour appears to creep in.

Keeping Watch

The first experience (that I can remember) was when I was expecting my daughter. I was due to give birth in a hospital which had been receiving some bad publicity concerning its maternity care and infant mortality. I was, understandably, rather worried about the impending birth.

One night, I awoke suddenly to find my grandfather standing at the side of the bed. Everything seemed clear, like daylight, and he looked just as I remembered him. My grandfather had lived with my family from when I was around six years old to sixteen, and as the oldest and the youngest, we understood each other and were close.

I didn't feel in the slightest bit frightened, and although there were no audible words I understood that he was reassuring me that everything was going to be okay and I should stop worrying. I then fell back to sleep, reassured, and the birth did go well. My daughter is now twenty-four and has a daughter of her own!

The second occasion was a while after my father's death. He adored his grandchildren (by then I also had a son). I was bathing them together, and they started to talk to me about ghosts and were frightening themselves, as children like to! I explained to them that the only person who would have a real interest in coming to see them was their grandad, but as he loved them so much he would never want to do anything to frighten them. At that a comb flew off the top of the bathroom cabinet into the washbasin. It had been kept in that place for years, and never just fell off of its own accord. The children and I both laughed that it was Grandad's way of telling us all that what I had said was exactly right – but none of us were frightened by it.

I also feel my father close to me when I've been decorating (something he was especially good at), and when I've finished a project and it looks good, I can feel him telling me that I've done a good job. However, I also feel his disapproval should I be tempted to take short cuts!

My most recent visit was when I was in great pain and spending a sleepless night due to a tooth abscess. I was all alone as my husband was working nights. On one of the occasions when I woke, I felt my grandmother was in the room with me. I had an oak toy chest, which my father had made for us when we were children, and it was placed in the corner of my bedroom. I just knew my grandmother was sitting on the chest, keeping a vigil. There was no one to see but I could feel her in the room. However, sometime later I went to see a clairvoyant, and he told me that I'd had a night visitor who'd been seated on a small chest with a padded top in the corner of my room! So it acted as a sort of confirmation to me.

I was also told by a clairvoyant that my dad had been with my son when he'd had a small accident in his car, and it brought tears to my eyes to know that my dad watches over the children and can see them growing up.

This classic 'watching over the family' is what our loved ones seem to do best. Their interest in their loved ones on THIS side does not seem to waver, even though their physical form may have changed to one of spirit rather than the body we are familiar with.

My friend Jewelle St James is the author of *All You Need Is Love*. Jewelle lives in Canada. She was kind enough to share her own story.

Goodbye Dad

My father was a spiritual man. Silver Birch and James Van Praagh were a few of his favourite truth seekers. Dad spent the last twenty years of his life studying the 'other side'. I always wondered if he was afraid of dying, or if he just sought the truth of the inner spiritual workings of our Universe. Maybe his motives for learning were a bit of both.

One summer's day in 2004, I suddenly felt an intense sadness. I drove on the highway leaving our town and headed towards the Rogers Pass, the gateway to the Rocky Mountains. I stopped by a green glacier-fed river, and began to weep. As I watched the strong rushing river, I knew my father was about to leave our planet. His life was slipping away, and I could no more stop it than halt the flow of the powerful aqua river.

I resumed life, and called my dad that night. All was fine, and I felt silly at my tears shed earlier that day. My dad lived in a care home, and had been there six months. On arrival his first request was that I buy him a tape recorder. He had his own message for the world, and he began a tape intended to spread the word to his fellow residents on what they could expect upon their death. He paused the tape player often so that he could find just the right words, and drew a graph to visually explain the dimensions on which they, as souls, would travel once they left the earth's sphere.

One afternoon in early August the phone rang; a call from the care home. Dad had fallen, broke his hip, and was being transported to the nearest hospital. Dad lived a hundred miles away so I could only spend the afternoon in a daze waiting for a call from his doctor. I walked in circles and passed the calendar on my kitchen wall. I wondered if Dad would live until his birthday in late August. I aimlessly looked out of the window at a train in the distance. I could see words written in spray paint on the side of a box car: THE END.

The sinking feeling in my stomach told me I was receiving a message and to be prepared. The news from the doctor verified the message. Dad not only had a broken hip but brain tumours were discovered.

Members of the family came to say their goodbyes, and Dad reported that all his daughters had been to see him. 'Konni' too had come, Dad had said, although she had passed away four years earlier …

I can't remember the series of events, but my younger sister Korinn and I began realizing our father's connection to native spirituality (Dad's heritage is Scandinavian). We already knew he thought the Native Americans had the right idea of spirit, but as his time came near, we were intuitively being shown just how strong that connection was.

I had a 'dream', where a native man said to me matter of factly, 'The elders are on their way for Henry.'

My sister was the last member of our family to visit

Dad. As she travelled to the hospice she saw six or seven eagles circling above an Indian reserve; a place where Dad often attended a yearly pow-wow. Dad always commented on how every year a lone eagle circled high above the pow-wow. To see so many eagles circling was an unusual sight.

Upon arriving at the hospice Korinn saw an eagle feather lying on Dad's chest. A dream catcher with feathers was on the nearby wall, that Korinn had brought earlier, but there was no way a feather could have travelled from the wall to Dad's chest. No earthly reason, that is ...

Dad had even been aware enough to see the feather and asked that she leave it there.

Korinn left the hospice in tears knowing she would never see our dad again. As she and her husband turned on to the highway they passed a van with written words on the side, 'Lasting Memories', which she also took as another message.

Dad passed away the next morning, a week before his birthday.

I have since discovered the significance of an eagle feather lying on one's chest; I read that the feather is a sign that the elders were taking Dad back to the great White Spirit.

This great sadness at losing a loved one was blessed by the amazing and meaningful passage to the other side and the secure knowledge that Jewelle's father was being collected and safely escorted.

Losing a loved one at any time is terribly sad but I am constantly amazed at how they have the ability to bring back humour from the other side. Jane told me her story a long time ago and I had intended adding it to a magazine article – it seems that 'the story' preferred to be added to my book as it turned up in the wrong file … so here it is!

Doorbell

My brother passed away five years ago, which was hard as we were very close. About a year after he had passed away, I fitted a cordless doorbell to my door. Well, after about a month the doorbell would ring at all times of the day and night. Whenever I went to check no one would be there.

One day I had just let someone out and immediately the doorbell rang. 'Ha!' I thought, 'Got you now,' and I immediately opened the door again, but – lo and behold no one was there.

As I stood there the doorbell began to ring 'ding-dong'. I was mesmerized because I wasn't touching it but yet it was still ringing. My husband came to see what I was playing at. 'It's not me,' I said and he stood there in shock as the doorbell continued to ring.

After a while, someone broke the bell button down-stairs so you couldn't push it and I removed it but left the base upstairs on the wall. A few months after that, the doorbell began to ring again ... all on its own! I wasn't frightened, but somehow knew it was my brother communicating, just to let me know he was there. In a way it was quite comforting.

Well, about four or five months ago, after about two years without a 'ring', the doorbell rang. My elder son was here and he looked shocked. I knew it was my brother but wondered why he'd rung. Before I went to sleep that night, I asked him, if it was him, would he come to me in my sleep and let me know what he wanted?

At 1.18 am the 'doorbell' woke up the whole household with its continual ringing! I had to get up and take it down to stop it. When I woke up the following morning, I just laughed to myself as I knew it was my brother playing games. 'Coincidentally', this was also the exact time of his passing.

When I asked him to come to me, I meant in a dream, but he was always the joker and decided to do it his way. Even now when I think about it, I can just see him laughing at his 'funny' joke.

This is not the only time he's 'visited' me; he often gives me spiritual hugs and I know when he's around me. I will always miss him, but I know he's only a heartbeat away. God bless you, Phil. I love you.

This grandad also had a sense of humour and took the opportunity of reminding everyone of his earthly love of fish and chips!

Fish and Chips

One night after my grandfather had died I awoke to the strong smell of fish and chips in the bedroom. The smell was so real and so strong that I had to get out of bed and go and check in the kitchen to see if anyone was in the house eating fish and chips ... they weren't!

When Emma's husband passed over it was a complete shock to the whole family, but she believes that their love, their meeting and their whole life together was part of a bigger plan which was pre-ordained.

Her husband Andy continues to show that he is around her. I'll let her share her moving story.

Loving Husband Comes Back Again ...
and Again ...

On the night of Tuesday 15 July, Andy, my husband, a fit and healthy man, died suddenly and unexpectedly at home from a brain seizure. He was four weeks short of his thirty-seventh birthday.

Looking back now, I believe that his destiny was fore-told with spirit intervention. The things that happened could not all be coincidences.

We met, 'by fate', in 1991, at a function that he de-cided to attend at the very last minute after a neighbour invited him. I had also decided to go at the very last minute with my friend's sister, as my friend, Emma, was unable to go. I know that if Emma had been with me, I would not have given Andy my correct telephone number when he asked me later on that evening.

We soon became 'a couple', and like most couples we had our nicknames. He was my 'alligator', and I was his 'angel'. In fact he called me by that name more than any other.

In August 1996 we married and I vowed to become his 'angel' for life. I walked down the wedding aisle to the tune of 'November Rain' by the group Guns 'n' Roses. I know it's not exactly your normal wedding music, but the instrumental beginning is very moving, and we were, as Andy liked to call us, a couple of 'old rockers' , so it seemed to suit us both.

In 2001 Ben, our second son, was born, but the week following his birth, the company Andy worked for went into liquidation and he became unemployed. Andy was never one to brood and he soon picked himself up. He decided to set up his own business, Complete Wood-work. At first it was hard, but we soon moved into the swing of self-employment life, and the diary became booked solid and the business did well.

The Friday before Andy's death, I visited my parents' house with our two boys. Ben, who had just turned two, decided to rearrange the ornaments and pictures. He very carefully moved a photograph of Andy and I, taken on our wedding day, but as he put it down the glass cracked in the frame. There was one solid crack straight through Andy's head. At that time we thought nothing more of it and just placed the photograph in a drawer for safekeeping.

The night Andy died I was supposed to have been out. My scheduled meeting was cancelled at the last minute because one of the other people involved had been signed off from work, and felt too ill to make it. That person was my mother. Had my meeting not been cancelled I would have arrived home too late to even attempt to save Andy's life, and to the possible scenario of one of my sons finding him dead. Although it was still awful, at least I was with him when he passed. Obviously, the rest of that night was spent in a daze, but things started happening the following evening.

Early Wednesday evening I had returned home with Mum, to collect some personal belongings. We decided to stay at my parents for a while. On the return journey my mother asked if I had 'seen' Andy since he had passed, and we discussed the fact that my grandfather 'Pop Pops' had visited the family after he passed.

Just as we pulled up onto her driveway my mobile phone 'bleeped' at me. The keylocked phone was in my bag, in the footwell of the car. Thinking it was rather strange, I removed the phone to see that it was displaying a message advising me that I had 'no voice match', the message you receive when you try to 'voice-cue' a number. Obviously I hadn't done this and the phone was keylocked and in my bag anyway. The only person I have programmed into my phone for this service is Andy, which seemed rather a strange coincidence after our conversation in the car!

In the twelve days preceding his funeral more strange occurrences happened. My mobile, once again, displayed a message, Andy's date of birth, only this time the phone had been turned off. One of the boys' toys, a 'laptop computer' decided to say hello and bleep even though it was closed and therefore effectively turned off. Even after it had been opened, turned on then off, closed and put away, it still continued to say hello intermittently during the time that my mum was sat on her own and feeling emotionally bereft ...

Another strange thing happened when my brother-in-law and I had a heated argument whilst we sat in the garden. The area around where we sat turned into a cold, windy hurricane, yet the rest of the garden was still and warm. We also had the strong scent of Stargazer lilies surround us. Stargazer lilies are the only flowers I ever bought for the house, so they meant a lot to me.

The garden at the time was full of family ... but no Stargazers were in sight.

There was one moment of humour. I was sitting and wondering, 'What do you wear to your husband's funeral?' Then when I looked up from my seat I saw a lady wearing a shocking pink t-shirt with the superman emblem! Andy had this emblem tattooed on his shoulder, and had arranged to have the emblem made into a silver pendant as one of his first gifts to me. I went and bought the t-shirt!

I remember when I entered my empty house to clean it on the day of the funeral. The strong smell of cigarettes hit me as I entered. Andy and I both smoked, but only in the garage, and anyway I hadn't been home for a cigarette and the only other person to have visited briefly was the cat-sitter, and she hadn't smoked in the house!

I had been on anti-depressants for two years leading up to the event, and couldn't even decide what flavour crisps to eat. I found I had been given an inner strength, as if someone was holding me up at my shoulders and helping me to deal with everything. At the funeral I knew I wanted to read and what to read, I knew that Andy wouldn't have wanted hymns, but certain records (once again 'November Rain' was played) and signs that meant something between the two of us. It was strange, I knew where the records and CDs that I needed would be, yet as Andy used to do mobile discos, they could have been anywhere – in the loft, in the garage, in his workshop – but they were all on the shelf.

That 'strong helper' remained with me up until the day of the funeral, but as I had been pre-warned by a spiritual friend, 'he' would leave after the final words had been said. As I threw my red rose on top of the coffin my protector, strength and helper went too, but not for long.

There have been some arduous tasks to deal with since then; personal and emotional conflicts, form filling, birthdays, our wedding anniversary and more birthdays, but none have passed without a 'coincidence'. Visiting the cemetery on Andy's birthday I received a feather … a tiny white fluffy feather … but no birds from which they could have fallen were in sight.

On our anniversary, the boys and I went south to stay with family friends, trying to make the day less traumatic. Whilst we were there I phoned my mum on her mobile phone, only to discover that she was visiting Andy at the cemetery at that exact moment. After a few minutes I asked her to give him our love, and at that moment another feather floated down and landed at her feet.

I knew, therefore, that another day would be significant when I returned to my car after dropping Ben at nursery. I found another feather sitting on the roof of my car, but not blowing in the wind. It was as if it was being held there by something until I'd had the chance to pick it up.

On 8 September it was my son Tom's ninth birthday. His birthday card was one of those noisy cards that play a tune when you open them. His card played 'Happy Birthday to you'. Unfortunately, Ben snatched at the card so it stopped working. No amount of tweaking or fiddling would get it to play again, so it was closed and put on a shelf in the kitchen out of reach. When Tom had blown out the candles on his cake, he decided that he wanted to cut the cake himself. He picked up the knife and on the first cut the card started to play! After that, no matter how hard we tried we couldn't get it to play again, and in the end we had to return it to the shop.

A similar thing happened when I went upstairs to print off a document for a friend who was waiting downstairs. I turned the computer on and then noticed that an e-mail, sent to me over a month earlier by my brother-in-law, regarding his wish to purchase Andy's car and assist with payment of the funeral, had been printed out and was in the printer tray.

The latest thing to happen was finding a record that I didn't even know existed. Whilst sorting through boxes of records in the loft, I found a twelve-inch picture disk of our song 'November Rain'. The picture on the front, back and cover slip is of an angel!

Many other small things have happened. I often see his reflection in the glass, but when I move to look closer it's gone. I also hear the little cough he used to make. I am also aware that a cynic would say that it's the mind

playing tricks or brain imprinting. Coincidence? Spirits?
Andy? Angels? I know what I think!

And I know what I think too!

CHAPTER 11

Warnings from the Other Side

The first question which the priest and the Levite
asked was: 'If I stop to help this man, what will
happen to me?' But ... the good Samaritan
reversed the question: 'If I do not stop to help
this man, what will happen to him?'

Martin Luther King Jr

The soul is eternal.

Edgar Cayce

One phenomenon which always intrigues me is the
way our loved ones seem able to communicate warnings for us from the afterlife. I once asked why and I
believe that sometimes our relatives and friends on the
other side are helping a little more than maybe they
should! Why they do this I am not sure but I know that
many people are grateful for their intervention just the
same. Our loved ones may not be concerned that a life
difficulty that we are going through is part of a lesson.

They want to help us and ease our difficulties even if it is against the spiritual rules.

In times of danger it is perhaps easier to believe and understand a presence with which we are most familiar. Would you be more likely to listen to the sound of your loving grandmother in the afterlife or a strange voice you do not recognize? Naturally, the familiar is going to be more easily accepted in perilous situations.

This next story is one of my own. My uncle in spirit is a regular visitor to many in the family. He appears in dreams and visions and flickers lights when he attends family occasions. I had to be pretty sure that his advice was correct before I suggested to other family members to heed his advice. You will see the frightening predicament we were in. But he has advised me from the other side before and his advice is always sound.

I'll let you read the story.

Dream Warnings – DON'T Have the Operation

Our extended family had arranged a big holiday in Spain with the three individual families, even though my father had been ill in the weeks before our trip.

'Don't worry Mum,' we reassured her. 'If Dad is taken ill we will deal with it if or when it happens. I'm sure everything will be fine.' There would be six adults altogether in the two villas, so plenty of help if we needed it.

The holiday was great. Two weeks in Nerja, an area

we knew well. As always, we planned to go out for dinner on our final night. We always went to an amazing Italian restaurant in Nerja itself, but this time I felt that something was wrong. The night before, I slept restlessly, and had a strange visitation dream where my uncle Eric appeared to me. It had happened before, and he was always a source of helpful advice. The message was clear: 'Don't let your dad have the operation to treat his gall stones.' As far as I knew, there were no plans for my dad to have an operation but I shared my 'dream' experience with other members of the family the next day just the same.

We had to be out of our villas early in the morning of the final day so we planned a last night out together at the Italian restaurant. Our giant pastas and pizzas arrived amongst much giggling and laughter, but after only two or three mouthfuls we noticed that Dad looked poorly.

'Are you okay?' I asked.

'Just a little cold,' said Dad, and he was visibly shaking. Someone put an extra jacket over his shoulders but he was clearly not well. Waiters flapped around Dad and brought him a glass of water. Could they ring for a doctor? Was it something to do with the food? We needed to get him out of there!

Dad was virtually carried down the sixty or so steps back to the villa and started to be sick, but Mum seemed in control and shooed us all out of the way. In the early hours of the morning I received a call on my mobile.

'We're ringing for an ambulance or something because your dad has been vomiting all night and is really dehydrated.'

Struggling to find a suitable emergency number I remembered the dream. 'We need to ask for help,' I said calmly, looking skywards, and almost immediately we found an English-speaking doctor's number from the pile of helpful notes on the table. We called him and he arrived very quickly, but decided to call an ambulance.

My mum wrote out a large cheque to cover the consultation fee and climbed into the ambulance with Dad. At least the hospital was expecting us and would know what was wrong.

The ambulance sat there for what seemed like forever. A different doctor arrived and amazingly, she also spoke a little English, but we struggled to communicate. Why were they not rushing him to the hospital?

We seemed to wait out in the early dawn for such a long time. It was so cold. They were trying to stabilize him before driving off, so there was nothing we could do to help ... or was there? We began to ask for the angels to help us and almost immediately they were ready to leave. We were left bewildered.

I made a quick telephone call to England to update our two other sisters before looking at my watch. It was nearly time for breakfast and yet I still hadn't been to sleep. A tear dropped down my face. I think for the first time I realized that Dad's life was in danger. Our plane was due to fly back to England that very afternoon. Would we all be on that plane? It now seemed unlikely.

We had suitcases to pack from both villas, rubbish to clear, and we still had to sign out of our accommodation and hand over the keys, and all this before we could follow to the hospital. An hour later we drove to the site office to hand over the keys. The front gated area was open and confidently we walked through, but immediately the security alarms began to blare out. The site office itself was closed and no one was around to take our keys. We would have to drive the hour to the hospital and then come back later to hand over the keys and check ourselves out. We drove away with the alarm ringing in the background. I felt overwhelmed with stress and grief.

We got out the map to try and work out our route. Did anyone know which way to go? What was the name of the hospital again? Someone remembered seeing hospital signs near to the airport so we headed off in that direction and hoped for the best. We got lost several times on the way and even when we got to the hospital we drove down a side road instead of travelling to the main entrance.

Dianne and I got out whilst our husbands tried to find a way of parking. Was this the right hospital? We'd forgotten to ask the angels! We waited in the queue at reception but of course the man on reception couldn't speak English, which was seriously not his fault! I wrote down Dad's name on a piece of paper and drew a picture of an ambulance. Was I indicating the universal symbol for 'Is my dad at the hospital?'

The receptionist gave no indication that he had understood and I assumed he was going to check for us, so we moved back and waited, and waited, and then waited some more! Were we even at the right hospital? We still had no idea.

We walked sheepishly back over to the reception desk and the man looked at us crossly. Had we done something wrong? He waved us into a side room as I showed him the piece of paper with my father's name on it again and he shoved it back at me, crossly pointing to the waiting room. We still had no idea if Dad was in this hospital and we'd now waited another whole hour. We just about had enough money for a drink each from the machine so we sat and waited some more.

Terrified and concerned, we walked back out to reception and another large queue had formed. We'd forgotten to ask the angels for help, hadn't we. Could Uncle Eric or the angels help us? A man was watching us curiously from the other side of the reception and started to walk over. I couldn't believe it ... he spoke English! He apologized for listening to our conversation but explained that he was a patient and wanted to help us. We were ready to drop down on our knees with gratitude! Had the angels sent him? Thank goodness!

He immediately began an animated conversation with the scary man on reception and kept gesturing in our direction. His voice had great authority. A few minutes later he strode over. Dad was in the hospital and he was waiting to be examined. He was permitted to take us to see him. What a relief ... after all this time. And we now knew he was still alive.

We were led into a small room with trolleys crowded around. Each trolley contained a patient, each patient had at least one person with them, and all were being treated in this same space. Mum spotted us and the feeling was overwhelming as we explained what had been happening. So many patients, so many people, so much had happened.

Our 'guide' stayed with us to act as interpreter for over four hours. I told him, 'You're our angel,' and was not surprised when he pulled out a pendant which was hidden under his shirt – it was decorated with two angels! He too believed in angels.

Each problem was followed by a request from us to the angels and each time the problem was overcome quickly in some 'co-incidental' way. The hospital wanted to admit Dad to the hospital, and they wanted him to stay. He needed further tests and probably an operation. An operation? NO! He was not to have an operation; Uncle Eric had warned me in the dream.

After yet another request, another English-speaking doctor appeared. We couldn't believe it! Today was not even his normal day apparently. (Thanks Uncle Eric, thanks angels.)

'Could we please take Dad home?' If we left within the next hour we might make our plane, we explained. We could all fly home together. We silently prayed.

Miraculously, they agreed to all of our demands ... as long as we signed release papers. They wouldn't be held responsible if anything went wrong. In less than two minutes someone walked in with the injection he needed and we all rushed off to the airport.

Dad was so weak that we had to hold him up in the wheelchair whilst we pushed him down the corridor. The airport was still an hour's drive away and we still had to return the villa keys. You're doing the right thing, you can do this, I heard clearly in my head.

It was a long flight but we had the angels with us and each problem was resolved almost immediately on request. We were going home, it was what he and all of us wanted.

Investigations showed that he had a blockage, gall stones. Amazingly, back in the UK, the doctors sorted the problem without cutting him; we were all so relieved. The doctors felt he would have been far too weak to have made it through an operation. We knew we had done the right thing. Uncle Eric had shown the way and the angels had protected us safely from the other side.

Here is another person's story of a dream warning. Many people ask for help with healing from their angels and loved ones on the other side. Not everyone receives such clear guidance as in these stories and I believe that when a strong guidance does not come then the choice is totally ours. Sometimes there is not only one way or one appropriate outcome, just one of several paths – and we have to pick which path to walk. Sometimes the outcome is the same, whichever way we walk. Sometimes there is no perfect right or wrong answer … just a choice.

I totally trusted the source of my own message but you have to follow your own inner, 'gut' instinct. Remember always that we have free will and must decide many things for ourselves. I do feel that our loved ones on the other side do have some insight into what is coming up for us but if you didn't trust Uncle Frank when he was alive you might want to consider carefully his advice now he's passed!

Barbara was pretty sure of her own communicator!

DO Have the Operation

I had a dream where I saw my cousin telling me to tell his father to have the heart operation that had been suggested to him at the hospital.

My Uncle John had been diagnosed with a serious heart condition and he was absolutely terrified of having the operation. To make matters worse, he was told that there was only about a fifty per cent success rate. It was also a tricky procedure because his health was in bad shape as he suffered from bad asthma. He'd already decided not to have the operation, so it was difficult for me to intervene but I felt that I had to mention the 'dream' just the same.

I 'dreamt' Morris, (John's son) came to me, but he appeared as the man he would now be had he lived and grown up on the Earth. He told me to tell his dad he must go ahead with the operation, not to be scared and that all would be all right. He kept stressing that I must tell him.

In the morning I woke feeling very anxious. I also felt a little dubious about ringing my aunt as I knew they had agonized over their decision. It seemed strange that I should have been told about this via Morris (someone I never even thought about now).

To cut a long story short, my uncle did go ahead with the operation and it was a success. He said he had definitely made up his mind that he was not going to have it done. But when he heard about my dream he just knew it would be all right and that it was a sign. He went on to live a fairly healthy and active life for a good many years after his operation.

Lisa is used to regular visits from her nan, and on one occasion she feels her nan and her great nan even saved her life. With such clear evidence, it is hard not to believe.

This story has a strange twist in that it is similar to the three stories in the first chapter of Part 1, where other people report being lifted up into the air and placed into a position of safety. The slight difference here is that Lisa knew the lifting was being done with the assistance of her nan, who in this case was acting as her guardian angel.

Lifted IV

I often talk to my nan in my head when I go about my day. I was crossing the road one day, in a bit of a day-dream, but talking to her as usual, when I heard my nan call my name. I was just about to step off the pavement but the voice made me turn round, and I felt myself being pulled onto the path ... At the same time, an ambulance sped past me, right where I would have been standing. Nan pulled me from the path of a speeding ambulance just in time.

I thanked her, for saving my life, and told her she obviously did not want me with her right now! I hear my nan sometimes in the house and she often calls my name. I turn to look but obviously there is no one there, but I know it's her.

Lisa's story doesn't end here and she has had several strange but helpful contacts from her nan.

Helpful Visitors

I lost twins about two and a half years ago. At the time I asked my nan to guide them to her on the other side and to wait for them at the gates. One evening I was trying to sleep and I asked Nan to let me hear my boys speaking. I heard, 'Mum it's us, don't be afraid, we have come,' which was amazing.

Another occasion, I rang a clairvoyant and she asked me who was trying to trace our family tree. I was not sure but she said that there is one missing part of the puzzle and this could be found in Mum's bureau hidden under some paperwork, and that this message had come from Margaret (my nan). I rang my mum who told me that my sister was doing our family tree. My sister followed the instructions and found exactly what she had been looking for.

Sometimes I ask my nan to show me a sign that she is around me and my lights will flicker, and even on occasions my kettle turns itself on, or the television will turn itself off.

My great nan used to watch over us from the other side too. It was 6 December 1970 and my great nan had died a year earlier to the day. My mum woke to see her standing over my bed and when Mum asked her what was wrong, she said, 'Get her to the hospital – she is ill and it is not her time yet.'

At the time we lived in Brighton and although I had

difficulty breathing, Mum thought it might be asthma. Anyway, Mum took me to the doctor who referred us to Guy's hospital in London. They discovered that I had heart problems and needed immediate surgery to correct the problem. I had to spend six months in hospital and am glad to say I have had no major problems since.

Karen feels that her nan saved her life too, although even she has to admit that she has to take some of the blame!

Saved from a Fire

I am a smoker and one night I awoke in the early hours. Before going back to sleep I lit up a cigarette in bed (as I often do). The ashtray was on my husband's side of the bed so I lay on my side with my arm across him so I could reach it.

I must have fallen asleep as the next thing I remember I was burnt on the back off my leg (only a very quick touch) and I woke up with a start!

I realized that my cigarette had burnt right down. Thank goodness I had woken up. I sat up to put the end of the cigarette into the ashtray and I felt something touch my leg underneath and again I felt a quick burn. When I lifted up my leg I saw another lit cigarette, only it wasn't the one I had been smoking. It was half smoked (as if someone had touched me with it to wake me up then dropped in onto my bed). I picked up the cigarette and put it out. It had no tip on the end like my own cigarettes, it was a ready-made one like a 'Woodbine' or 'Park Drive', like my nan used to smoke!

Even I was shocked and although it sounds unbelievable, I still have the evidence to this day. There was no burn mark on my bedding and where it touched my skin it didn't continue to burn as it was just a slight touch, enough to make me jump and wake me up. I didn't even have a red mark. But to this day I thank whoever it was every day for stopping a disaster.

CHAPTER 12

Knocking on Heaven's Door

There is only one path to Heaven.
On Earth, we call it Love.

Anon

Heaven means to be one with God.

Confucius 551–479 BC

How many people have seen the pearly gates and returned? With the advance of modern technology, millions of people are now being brought back from the very brink of death and then continue to live a normal life. Well, I say 'normal' but of course, people see such wonders that they often do not want to return to our earthly world. In this chapter I want to deal with stories of people who have visited heaven and come back again ... even if in some instances it was only for a brief visit!

Some people pass over and then come back to reassure others that they are okay and even to share some of what they have seen and experienced once they passed.

Sharon had an experience which literally took her to the other side and back. The story is comforting in that Sharon, like many others, had been to heaven and loved it so much she wanted to stay.

Millions of people have had near-death experiences. During these experiences, it is common to see passed-over loved ones, hear celestial music, see amazing landscapes and beautiful crystal buildings. Often we see colours which are not of this earth, as Sharon did.

Cherry Tree

There are some days when we know everything is going to go wrong. This day I should have noticed the warning signs, but for some reason I ignored them.

It was just like any day really, but the only difference was that I was booked into a hospital to have my wisdom teeth taken out. I wasn't worried. Hospital was the easy way out because I had a terrible phobia against dentists.

My husband and son accompanied me to the hospital. My son was just two at the time, and we had decided if we let him see where I was going to be, he wouldn't worry. We arrived at the hospital early in the morning and went to the reception desk, booked in and went up to the ward. A nurse up on the ward took us to my bed, told me to get changed and get into bed, and then she left. I looked at the bed, then at my husband, and said, 'They have got to be joking.' The bed was only about four feet long. My legs would hang out of the end of the bed!

The nurse seemed cross with me because I hadn't got into the bed by the time she came back. My husband was making jokes about the bed, coming up with ways for me to fit in it. The nurse rushed off laughing loudly – it turned out that she thought it was for 'the little one'. Apparently I had been booked into the wrong ward!

My husband and son left, and I settled into the ward. The rest of the day was pretty normal and I was prepared for the operation. Now it was just a matter of waiting for the pre med. Everyone told me that as soon as you have the pre med you don't know a thing till you wake up the next morning after the operation. This sounded good to me!

So I lay in the bed waiting for my turn. In fact I couldn't wait! I was the last one. It seemed an age but at last two nurses turned up at the side of the bed with the pre med.

'This may feel like a donkey has kicked you at first, but wiggle your toes and it will soon go,' the nurse on the left said.

Well, that was no lie, it did feel like a donkey had kicked me – a rather large donkey – so I wiggled my toes and it did go. I settled back into the bed and waited. Any moment now it was going to knock me out and I wouldn't remember a thing ... that's what everyone had told me.

Ten minutes passed and I still felt the same; in fact I was wide awake. A few more minutes passed, I was thinking to myself that they had lied to me, the only reason I was given this was so I couldn't run for it. When I see all those people that told me about the pre med and that you remember nothing ...

Two people then arrived. The young woman took the top of the bed and the man took the bottom and they started to push the bed through the hospital towards the operating rooms. Halfway there, they started to have words with each other. It was clear they were boyfriend and girlfriend and they had fallen out. Well, you just can't just lie there and listen, can you? I thought that some of what they were saying was very personal, and I couldn't work out why they had even started this fight when I was laying there awake on the bed listening.

'Life is too short to fight,' I said. 'The problem you have is such a little one, treasure each other ... little things like this really don't matter in this world if you love each other.'

The bed stopped dead and they turned to each other with a look of shock on their faces like they had seen a ghost.

'It's the pre med,' the boy said confidently.

Okay, I thought, I will keep quiet, but this pre med thing has not done a thing for me. The bed arrived at the operating theatre, we went in and I looked round. I was in a room with doors coming off it everywhere, and the doors were open. 'I hope there is nobody in there,' I thought; I nearly pass out watching operations on the television, without seeing them in real life. The bed was soon surrounded by people.

'You look nice and asleep,' said the doctor.

'What does he mean nice and asleep?' I thought. 'I am wide awake.'

'No I am not,' I replied.

'It's the pre med. I am going to give you this injection and count to ten, and before I reach ten you will be fast asleep and remember nothing.'

I felt a sharp pain and everything went black. I couldn't move or see, but I could hear everything they were saying.

'Great, they have taped my eyes up,' I thought, 'and tied me down. Now, why can't they see that I am not asleep?' They went on chatting as if nothing was wrong. They talked about the things they were going to do that night and passing instructions about the operation backwards and forwards.

My god, I thought, nobody has listened to a word I have said. I can't hang around here all through the operation! The next thing I remember was a pulling feeling on my body, and in a flash I was sitting in a garden under a cherry tree that was in full bloom. Actually, I was by a road on the side of a verge that was lined with cherry trees. Each one was perfect and led up to a hill in the distance. Flowers stretched for miles on either side of the road, they were every colour you could think of and some were colours that didn't even exist in this world. Coming off them was a haze of shimmering light.

I have never felt more at peace with myself, or alive, and my mind didn't even contain any thoughts. I was home, and bathed in more love than I had known for a long time. I just sat under this cherry tree and I knew I had come here often to sit. I loved the peace and warmth of this place. I didn't think this exactly, I just knew. There was not a thought in my mind, I was 'at one' with this garden. I was a part of it, and at the same time, it was a part of me.

How long I had been there I don't know, and when I heard my name being shouted, it sounded so distant, as if the voice was miles away; a universe away. I didn't care. I was alive, I was me again. The voice called again and again, and I stood up and shouted, 'NO!' as loud as I could.

There is no way I am going back, I am home, leave me alone. The voice called again, and again I said, 'NO!' and each time my name was called you could hear more and more worry in the voice.

'There is no need to worry,' I shouted, 'I am home and safe. Now go away and leave me alone.' I turned and sat down under the tree.

That was when another voice spoke to me. The voice was a man's.

'You made your choice, and now you have to go back.'

'What do you mean I made my choice?' I replied.

'Before you were born you were asked to be shown this, you needed it so you could remember.'

'Why do I need to remember it?'

'Because your life will change. This will always prove to you that life goes on, it never ends. Before you were born you set out in your life this moment; you even ensured that if you wished your life on earth to end at this moment it would … just as you set out in that plan. But you have chosen to go back,' said the voice.

Well I thought to myself, that's easily fixed.

'I have changed my mind, I want to stay.'

'This plan was made at a soul level. All you had to do was to walk over that hill and you would have remained here. If you stayed seated under the tree, your life went on and you returned. You may not understand why right at this moment in time, but as you get older things will all fall into place.'

Now came the part when I put every two year old to shame.

'Well you can't make me go back,' I shouted.

The voice in the distance calling my name was getting more and more desperate. If this was some wise soul in the world of spirit on the other side, trying to get me to return, they must have had a quiet giggle to themselves. Never ever, if you find yourself over there, say, 'You can't make me go back.' They have ways of doing that, and they're very good.

All of a sudden this thought popped into my head, 'Remember your husband and son,' and this was followed by their names. 'They need you.'

I have never felt guilt like it my whole life, not before or since. It was so strong, it brought me to my knees. Then I felt myself falling, then a jerk in my body, and my eyes opened. I was back in my body and I was not happy about it.

I sat bolt upright and looked at the nurse that had been shouting my name, and boy was I angry.

'What did you bring me back here for?' I shouted.

There was a look on the nurse's face, that said in a silent way, 'I have heard about people doing this, or read about them, now I am face to face with someone who has just experienced it ...'

Seconds before I had been knocked out by a general anaesthetic, now I was sitting there looking her in the face, wide awake, as if I had not even had one.

My bed was pushed back and I remained silent, but the odd thing was that noises and voices were loud, and I mean loud. They nearly shattered my eardrums. As I arrived back in the ward, everyone else was out cold. I was getting some odd looks from the nurses and I know that I was meant to still be asleep! Every time I closed my eyes, the cherry tree and the garden popped back into my mind. I just wanted to go back there. I felt terribly homesick, and the loud noises didn't help.

When I left the hospital, nothing seemed to take the feeling away. I had a son and a husband I loved dearly, but I just wanted to go 'home', back home to my real home, not this place here. For months this went on. Eventually, my hearing returned to normal, but I still had this longing, and more than that I wanted to find this place. Where was it? What was it? How did I get back?

Deep in my heart I knew the answers. I was born with one foot in this world and one in the next. I had always wanted to see the world of spirit and now when it had happened, all I wanted to do was to return.

The day it all changed was odd. My husband and I were out shopping and he knew about my love of books on psychic matters. We were in a second-hand book-shop when he called me over because he had spotted an interesting book. The book was called *Life in the World Unseen*, by Anthony Borgia, and I got such a shock when I started reading it … the cherry trees, the flowers, the road and the hill; they were all there.

I made my mum read it, and my husband; in fact everyone had to read it. How can I sit in a place that was described in a book? The book was written when I was so young, and yet until that day I had never seen it or known it existed.

The story in this book was told by the spirit of a man from the 'other side'. This book at the time was very rare to find, and it's only in the last few years that it has been reprinted. I can imagine that this is due to the joy it has brought so many people, and loads of people borrowed my copy, then pestered the publisher to print it again.

Some people may say I had a dream that day, others will say the medication caused the experience. I am now a parapsychologist and psychic counsellor and I challenge any expert anywhere in the world to give me an answer to that question.

Even to this day, when I close my eyes I can see those flowers, but I just can't put into words what some of those colours are. The colours do not exist in this world, and even if I tried to recreate them I couldn't, it's impossible. How can my mind create something that doesn't exist? I feel so lucky to have glimpsed the other side.

I did need that experience. Everyday I learn lessons that would take many lifetimes to learn, but I know one day I will sit under that cherry tree again and be free. This life is but a short time in our existence. I sit in an internet chatroom and help people discover the world of spirit. I use my experience to unite them with loved ones that have passed over. I want to give them hope and understanding, but more than that, to help them to once again to 'believe'.

In the words of Anthony Borgia, there are few people who have not at times wondered what happens after death. To discover what the next world is like we must in fact enquire of someone who has been there. If I have brought a measure of comfort or of good hope, then great is my reward.

I have read hundreds of accounts of what lies beyond heaven's door. The beautiful gardens and colours 'not of this world' feature regularly. No matter how many times I read about these stories, I always want to read more. In fact, I managed to track down a copy of the book that Sharon mentions in her account and I am reading it right now!

Moving on then. When Gemma was ill in hospital she found herself in an altered state where she was able to communicate with both her father and her grandfather who were both on the other side.

Chatting with Dad and Granddad

My dad passed away when I was just ten years old and then shortly afterwards my grandfather passed away too. I miss them very much but they have both visited me since they passed over. I have had several conversations with them in my dreams which seem so real it was extraordinary.

I had a spell in hospital where I was critically ill. At one point I was speaking to both of them and they told me what Mum was saying to my stepdad whilst she was at the opposite side of the hospital. Later I was able to recite exactly what my mum was saying to him. I repeated this to my mother who nearly passed out with shock!

Janey's sister is the one who said goodbye to her after she had passed over in a sudden and very tragic car accident. I know she found it a great comfort. These stories of afterlife communication offer great changes in the people who experience them. The comfort aspect helps people to move on with their lives knowing that death of the physical body is not the end of life.

Sister Says Goodbye

When I was thirteen years old (I am now forty-seven) my younger sister, who was just eight, was hit by a speeding car. My sister Ann died but thankfully her friend did survive. My sister and I were very close and we looked so much alike. In fact, Dad used to call us 'twinnies' due to our similarities.

I wasn't allowed to go to her funeral. I had to stay home and look after my younger sisters but a few days after the funeral I saw her. I lay in bed one evening in the room we had shared together and I knew that something or someone was in the room with me. The sensation was very strong and I was terrified at the time. I lay there for a long time, too frightened to turn around or to call out. I was bathed in sweat and my heart was hammering in my chest. Eventually I plucked up the courage to look and as I turned around I could see my sister just standing there.

She was very solid and dressed in a bridesmaid's dress which I had never seen before. Ann was going to be a bridesmaid to my cousin on 14 February but was killed on 27 January. She was buried in her bridesmaid's dress. As soon as I realized it was her, the fear just disappeared. I actually heard her speak to me and she said, 'Please don't cry any more. I know you are sad and miss me but we will be together again one day and when that day comes it will seem like a moment.'

Sadly my mum never believed me. In fact I think she was angry about it. As an adult now, I realize why. I know how lucky I am to have had such an experience. Spiritually, it was the beginning for me and since then I have always believed that life continues after the physical body dies.

Pearl's mother came back to visit her shortly after she passed and then came again to support her daughter when she needed it the most.

Voices Through the Curtain

When my mother passed away in 1977, I saw her face above her casket. Then later at the cemetery I saw her standing in the middle of two men dressed in dark suits. She smiled at me and initially I thought I was going crazy when I saw her. I actually screamed out to one of my aunts and said, 'Oh my God I just saw mama.'

Then when I was seven months pregnant with twins I was put in hospital because the doctor was afraid I was going to lose them. That night in my room, my mother came to me. I saw a clear mist which I could see through. I remember looking around at the room and seeing a chair in the corner. The windows were right by my bed and the clear mist seemed to go from the chair to the side of my bed.

I remember saying, 'Mama, you didn't have to come.' And she replied, 'You knew I would be here.'

'But you had such a long way to come,' I said, but she answered me by saying, 'It's not that far ...'

The next morning the lady in the room with me told me she was scared to death during the night because she thought I had company. She said it was very late but she had heard voices from my side. I tried to put her mind at rest by telling her that I must have been talking in my sleep, but she said she had heard two different voices. She said that she even pushed the curtain back to see who was with me, and realized that no one was there. She was really scared!

My mother had always been with me when I'd had my other children so it was nice to know that she was aware of what was going on in my life after she passed.

Lorraine was very lonely after she lost her husband but she feels that he had more than a little to do with 'fixing her up' with someone new. Can our loved ones influence our life on this side from their heavenly homes? It seems that sometimes they can! Lorraine's story is another one which came to me through my website so I'll let her tell you in her own words.

My Husband Is a Matchmaker
from the Other Side

I was looking at your website and thought I'd send you my story about communication after death.

For two weeks before my first husband died, I would wake up every day singing, 'I believe I can fly.' I had never heard the song before and asked around and no one I asked knew what it was. The day after he died, my son was playing a CD and that song played – it is from the Space Jam CD. My husband and I had both earned our private pilot licences before we had children, and flying was meaningful to us. We played the song at his funeral. For months after his death, we heard that song everywhere we went.

I also had numerous experiences at home. The first night, I had the kids sleep with me, and I know we all stayed in bed. I was awake all night (at least it seemed like it). The next day, my neighbour said she had seen someone (she thought it was me) pacing back and forth in the living room in the middle of the night. I know it was my husband – there was no one else in the house except me and the kids.

I belonged to a kind of support group at the time; we called ourselves 'Soul sisters'. They met the week after my husband died and said that he had been with them spiritually. He told them that he had been in the bedroom upstairs and wasn't feeling well. He went downstairs and that is where he fell down. When I came home that day, I'd found him downstairs, I also found his housecoat upstairs on the floor in the bedroom he said he had been in. I hadn't told anyone about the housecoat but they knew because he had told them.

I also had several stained-glass birds hanging in my bedroom window. For the first month or two after he died, these birds would swing back and forth, back and forth – this usually happened just when I had gone to bed. The windows were closed and there was no one else in the room. On another occasion, a hanger in the clothes closet just kept swinging and swinging, and it happened for so long that I actually sat down on the bed to watch it.

Two months after he died, I was getting dressed one morning and I felt myself being pushed back onto the bed (I was alone in the room). The push was hard enough that I sat down. Then I felt a pulling on my wedding ring! I knew that he wanted me to take my wedding ring off! My neighbour, who was a widower, was coming over to help me refinish the garage door that day.

I am now married to that neighbour! By the way, my first husband also visited me one morning, to let me know he approved of me getting together with the neighbour. I have absolutely no doubt that my first husband was communicating with me after he died.

Of course, the communication doesn't have to come from someone we know. A friend of mine was thinking a lot about the late psychic medium Doris Stokes, and then one day Doris came to her in a 'dream' visitation. They sat, just the two of them, in classic 'visitation' style in a room with just two chairs – one each. They just chatted and Doris seemed to have been able to pick up the fact that my friend had been tuning into her energy by thinking about her.

This next story is similar. When public figures pass over, many people report communicating with their idols over the months and years following their passing and often with the thought 'why me?' This happened a lot with the late Princess Diana, and many people wrote books and articles about their communication with her.

Here is a story about another famous person. Freddy Mercury was the lead singer in the group Queen and his passing was mourned by many people all over the world. He sadly passed on 24 November 1991. Stephen was shocked that he was feeling so sad about Freddie and felt uncomfortable in sharing the experience he'd had after he passed. He was worried that others might ridicule his experience and he is not alone with this concern for good reason.

Stephen also wrote to me at my website and kindly agreed to my publishing his account here.

Freddie Mercury

Twenty-four hours after Freddie Mercury died I just couldn't believe he had gone. I was deeply upset and felt very emotional and was crying a lot. I wasn't in love with the man or anything, or a huge sycophantic fan. I just kept thinking, what a terrible shame never to hear such a fantastic voice again. I was really, really upset.

And then, the following night, as clear as day, I can still see it now, Freddie Mercury's face appeared in my dream and spoke directly to me and said, 'Don't worry about me, I'm okay now. Please stop worrying about me. I'm okay,' and from that moment on I felt like a huge emotional weight had been lifted off my shoulders.

I mean, there must have been hundreds, if not thousands, of people who felt the same way as I did and I kept thinking, 'Why me, it can't have been real,' but I am so sure that this wasn't something conjured up by the brain. I honestly felt he came to visit me to put my mind at rest. I felt him touch me and felt all my anxieties drain away.

You can't really tell this sort of thing to too many people and indeed I haven't, but when I saw the request on your website, and having read some of your words online, I felt as though I had to write.

It's been good telling this to someone who might actually understand what I am writing about.

Sue's friend told me about her own special story concerning her dear friend Ann. She told me that she will always treasure her experience.

Visits from My Friend

A wonderful friend of mine called Ann passed three years ago after suffering from breast cancer for twelve years. She was forty-eight years old and we had been friends since junior school. She couldn't get out much in the latter stages of her illness so I used to pick her up and bring her to my place for lunch and we always loved to watch the jewellery sales on the shopping channel.

I was with her, along with her family, on the night she passed, although when I went to visit her that evening none of us realized this would be her last night with us. Ann and I had made a pact a few days before that she would give me a sign to show me that there was an afterlife and that she was happy.

Before I left to visit on that last evening I set my video recorder to record *Coronation Street*. The next day, as I was drinking a coffee and thinking of her at home, I glanced at the video which strangely was set to the shopping channel. Curiosity got the better of me so I re-wound my video; it had recorded *Coronation Street*, but the satellite and video had then switched to the shopping channel – all on their own.

I took this as my sign and I was so happy that I burst into tears. Ann was useless at setting the video, so must have learnt some new skills since she passed!

Since then I sense her around a lot, and I know that her daughters have sensed her too. Her eldest became pregnant recently. This was not planned as she is single, but she decided to go ahead and keep the baby against her family's wishes. One day, when she and I were talk-ing about Ann on our way back from a shopping trip, Helen mentioned that she would love a sign from her mum just to make sure she wasn't cross about the baby.

A short while later we arrived back at my house. As we walked in through the front door my radio alarm clock started ringing. I ran upstairs to turn it off and no-ticed it was still set to go off at 7.20 am and the time now was 2.30 pm. We were very confused! I had to smile. I made us both a coffee, wondering how I could tell Helen about the alarm clock, when she again started speaking about her mum and baby, and lo and behold the alarm went off again.

I was able to turn to Helen and say, 'There's your answer!'

Needless to say my alarm clock has never gone off at the wrong time before or since that day, and I have to say it truly made Helen's day.

It amazes me how our loved ones are able to manipulate clockwork items, and even electrics. My own family has an uncle who always flickers the lights at family events, as I mentioned before. At my sister's wedding we all asked him if he would appear and show himself in some way. The wedding service was held in a lovely hotel and directly over where the bride and groom stood was a light … you guessed it, it flickered on and off all the way through the ceremony.

I went to visit my dad one day whilst my mother was at work. We were chatting about spirit and how they have the ability to show that they are around us by doing these things. I actually said to Dad, 'You wait until I leave, uncle Eric will do something to show that he is around.' Just a second after I stood up to leave, the smoke alarm gave a single bleep and we both burst out laughing. My dad checked the battery but it was a brand new one and it was fine – it never bleeped again so make of that what you will.

Lynda e-mailed me her story.

The Music Box

I never believed in visitations or visits from beyond the grave until my brother passed over. He passed in a tragic accident but he continues to send us messages.

My brother was a helicopter pilot. The night after his accident my distraught father was standing by my brother's car (he'd left it at my father's house). It was about 2 am and my mother and uncle joined my father to console him. All of a sudden a helicopter came and hovered right over them (flicking its lights off and on as my brother had always done when he flew overhead). They said they wouldn't have believed it if they hadn't experience it themselves – I mean, it seems a little bizarre doesn't it?

A few months later my mom was in bed, and unable to sleep. My poor father had left to go to the hospital because my uncle had just had a heart attack. As she was lying in bed she unexpectedly heard my brother call her, and she looked up and saw him standing at the foot of her bed! He walked around to her side of the bed, sat down and held her hand. She was able to talk to him but he only smiled and rubbed her hand. Then, as quickly as he arrived he was gone.

I was sleeping in the other room and Mum asked me to join her so she could tell me about what had just happened. It was wonderful. We sat and talked a while and then all of a sudden a music box, one that had to be lifted to play, started playing all on its own! I think my brother was letting me know that he was still with us. I could go on and on because there are so many stories. It has been ten years since he passed and we still get messages, in dreams, and in everyday life.

These types of stories are surprisingly common. Clocks are another fun way that our loved ones communicate with us and bring a little light to our grief. Karen shares her story.

Clocks

I've had two children who have passed on. My son Lewis passed ten years ago, and then my daughter Jenna seventeen months after that. I knew during both pregnancies that I would be attending their funerals (something that should never ever happen to any mother).

Within a few months of Jenna's death I was sitting watching TV when one of the drawstrings for my curtains started moving. I shouted at the cat, thinking that she was playing with it, but she was sitting by my side. The dog was sitting at my feet, so neither of them could have been anywhere near the curtains. At this point the drawstring was still moving. I went over to the window to check that it was shut before walking around the house to make sure that all the other windows and doors were closed. I'm convinced it was Jenna telling me she was still with me.

My mum has also had a number of visits from Jenna and Lewis. She was watching a television show called ...*Strange but True*? which covers a whole range of paranormal experiences, when a picture frame with photos of Lewis and Jenna flew off the television (it actually flew over an ornament which was in front of it), and landed on the floor.

Mum also collects clocks. Her favourites are the miniature brass ones. She frequently finds that the times are all different (despite making sure they are all correct), or they all stop working at the same time. Her small chiming wall clock had the chimes switched off yet every so often it chimes ... for no apparent reason!

Our loved ones and angels can also bring with them scents and smells. Flower smells are common, especially roses, gardenias and other strong-smelling flowers like lavender.

This is Stella's experience.

Roses

I smelt flowers after my grandfather passed over in August. Grandma and Grandpa raised me (although my grandma died twenty years before). I owe them so much and miss them both terribly. I often cry when I think of how much they did for me.

This morning, I smelled flowers from my room, towards the whole living room area and kitchen of my house. It lingered for about an hour. As soon as I picked up the scent I realized that Grandpa and Grandma were both visiting me and I prayed. I can only hope that when I talk to them out loud, they can hear me. When my grandma died I saw her appear in my room. She was telling me something, although I do not know what she said. She appeared as a moving light but with a flowing energy of light static on her sides.

On another occasion I could smell a different kind of rose scent although I cannot describe it, apart from saying that it smells like something from heaven, an antique rose smell ... it's very hard to describe. I cannot forget that lingering scent and even my co-worker told me the smell followed me around. It's not the ordinary kind of a rose smell. I'll never forget that.

Our loved ones can be very ingenious in the way that they communicate and are now using every method of modern communication at their disposal. Several stories have reached me over the years of loved ones communicating through the telephone. Here is one of them.

This story is very personal to Sheena but she is convinced that her dad rang her to say goodbye one last time.

Sorry to Leave You

A few days after my father died I was sitting chatting with my mother and a few relatives when the telephone rang. I answered it and a voice that seemed so very familiar was telling me how sorry he was to have had to go, but not to worry; everything would be fine. He said that he loved me and I must take care of Pearl (my mum) and tell her that he loves her so very much. He then said he had to go, told me he loved me once again and then said, 'Goodbye darling.'

During the conversation on the phone I was reasoning with myself that it could not be my dad, but all the time I knew it was his voice. My mouth had literally dropped open and by now my relatives were asking what was wrong. I told them that my dad had just called and I passed on his message. You can imagine we were more than a little surprised!

Since then I have had quite a few experiences and I know my father is behind them. It is just his way of letting me know that he is not far away and that he is watching over me. He had always said to me that if there was a way to contact me from the other side then he would, so I know Dad is just following up on his promise of contact.

Our angels come to us in all shapes and sizes, both angels from the other realms in the form of our passed loved ones, animal angels and God's own heavenly servants of light, and human angels. Amazing, miraculous experiences seem to happen at any time and to ordinary folks all over the world! Know that your own angels are watching over you and sending you their love from the other side.

If you are interested in learning more about your angels then ask them to communicate with you. Remember we have to give them permission to be involved in our lives. When you put out the word, they make themselves known.

I was running an angel workshop in Leeds. It was a special day with some lovely participants, but one thing stands out in my mind. One of the ladies came up for a chat afterwards and she told me that she had bought *An Angel Treasury*. She had enjoyed reading it so much that she continued reading late into the night, then fell asleep, woke up again and kept on reading until she finished the book. I remember doing the same thing myself when I first started learning about angels and remember the way that angels showed they were around following my angel exploration …

Her husband, who was a non believer at the time, had been asleep besides her. In the morning he woke up coughing.

'Are you all right?' she asked him.

'Yes', he said, 'I think I must have swallowed a feather!'

ABOUT THE AUTHOR

Jacky Newcomb is one of the UK's leading paranormal writers and angel experts. She has a great interest in angels, spirit guides, psychic children, afterlife communication and all things mystical and paranormal. She has had many paranormal and angel experiences during her own lifetime, many of which she shares here. She has studied a wide range of paranormal and psychic phenomenon and holds a diploma in psychic development. Jacky is also a Reiki Master.

Jacky is the author of *An Angel Treasury* and *A Little Angel Love*. Her work has featured in the UK's foremost paranormal and mystical magazines including *It's Fate, Fate & Fortune, Prediction* and *Vision*. In addition she has produced features and articles for many non-paranormal women's magazines in the UK and around the world including *CHAT, My Weekly* and *Woman's Own*.

She runs several mystical 'agony aunt' columns and receives hundreds of queries and questions about paranormal experiences to her website and in response to her magazine and newspaper columns.

Jacky has acted as a consultant on several paranormal shows and magazine features, and been interviewed on television programmes such as ITV's *This Morning* and LIVINGtv's *Psychic Live*. She is regularly interviewed on radio about her work.

Jacky is one of the presenters on the DVD *Angels* (for New World Music), and recorded several guided meditations for *Paradise Music*. Signed copies of Jacky's books and other products are available at:

www.gabrielmedia.co.uk.

Jacky runs an online angel and spiritual gift shop with her husband John and they live in England in a small Staffordshire village with their two daughters, their dog and ginger tom cat.

For more information about Jacky and her work, visit her website, or write to her via HarperCollins (77–85 Fulham Palace Road, Hammersmith, London W6 8JB), remembering to enclose a stamped addressed envelope if you want a personal reply. Or, to ensure a reply, try e-mail, which is much quicker (jackytheangellady@yahoo.com)!

Jacky welcomes your own angel and paranormal stories for publication in future books.

To contact Jacky online go to:

www.jackynewcomb.co.uk.